AUG     2023

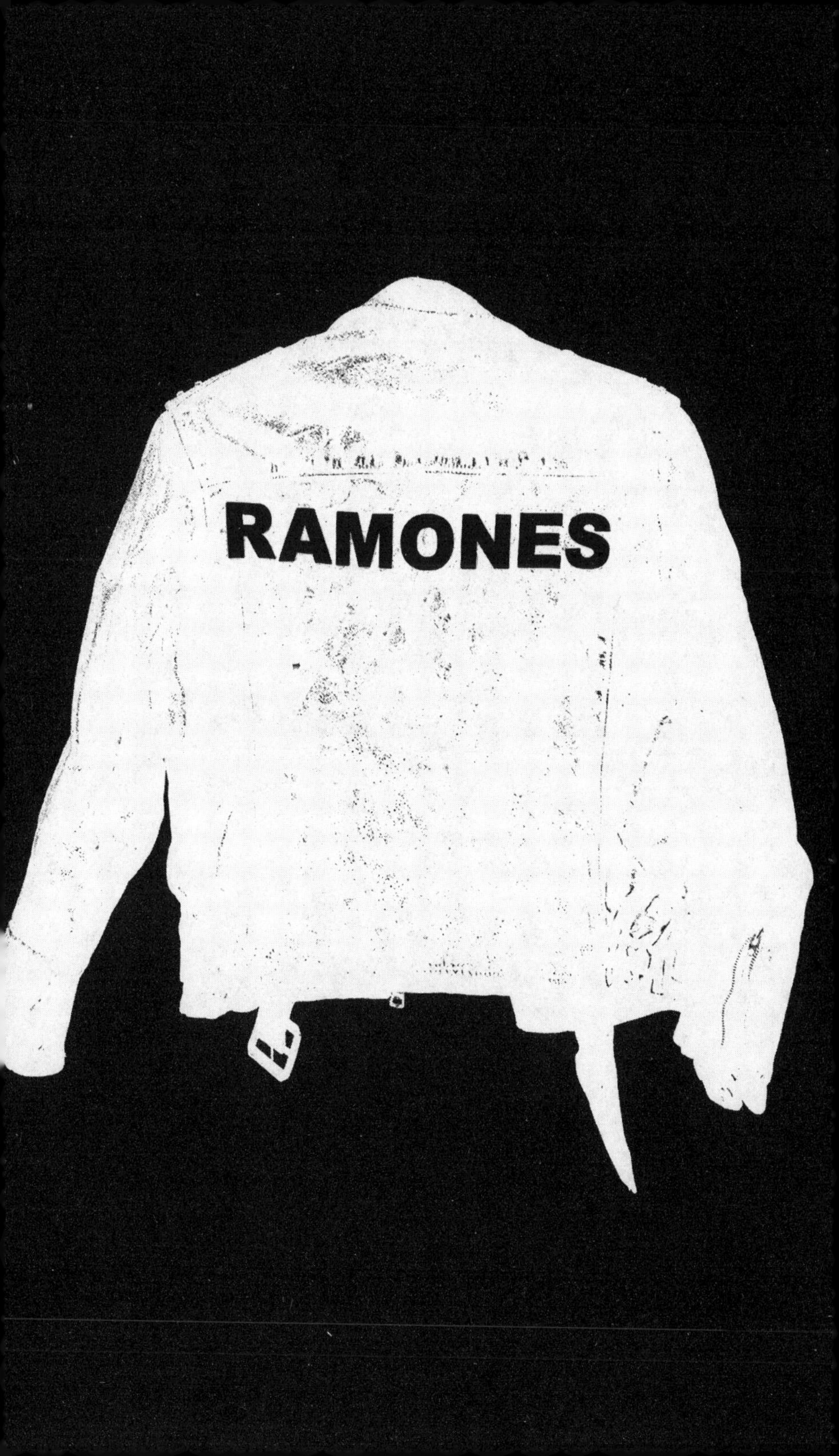
RAMONES

# GABBA GABBA HEY!
## A CONVERSATION WITH THE

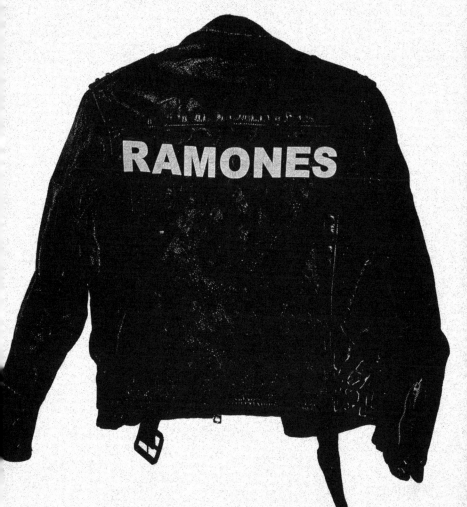

RAMONES

## CARL CAFARELLI

RARE BIRD
LOS ANGELES, CALIF.

RARE BIRD

THIS IS A GENUINE RARE BIRD BOOK

Rare Bird Books
6044 North Figueroa Street
Los Angeles, CA 90042
rarebirdbooks.com

For more information, address:
Rare Bird Books Subsidiary Rights Department
6044 North Figueroa Street
Los Angeles, CA 90042

Set in Minion
Printed in the United States

10 9 8 7 6 5 4 3 2 1

Library of Congress Cataloging-in-Publication Data available upon request

*For my lovely wife, Brenda, who had never heard the Ramones before we met. Within a few weeks, she was writing the lyrics to "Sheena Is a Punk Rocker" in the margins of her notebook. If that ain't love, I don't know what is.*

*IN MEMORY OF BONNI MILLER*
*This book couldn't have happened without you.*
*In memory also of JOEY, JOHNNY, DEE DEE, and TOMMY.*

# CONTENTS

# I BELIEVE IN MIRACLES
*Acknowledgments*

Aw, where to start? Big thanks to my former editor Jeff Tamarkin and my former managing editor Bonni Miller for the sheer magic they performed in presenting the original piece in 1994. Thanks to the Ramones' then-publicist Ida Langsam for arranging the interviews. And thanks, of course, to Joey Ramone, Johnny Ramone, Marky Ramone, and C. J. Ramone for being so generous in sharing their time and recollections with me.

Thanks also to my former colleagues John M. Borack, Greg Loescher, Ken Sharp, and Maggie Thompson for their advice and encouragement. Thanks to Steve Coulter for introducing me to Tyson Cornell and Rare Bird Books, and thanks to Tyson and his entire Rare Bird team (including Alexandra Watts, Hailie Johnson, and Kellie Kreiss) for making this dream come true.

When I did these interviews in 1994, there weren't a lot of Ramones reference books available. I made enthusiastic use of Jim Bessman's book *Ramones: An American Band* (St. Martin's Press, 1993). As the importance of the Ramones has become more widely recognized, Bessman's book has been supplemented by Monte A. Melnick and Frank Meyer's *On the Road with the Ramones* (Sanctuary Publishing, 2003), Mickey Leigh and Legs McNeil's *I Slept with Joey Ramone: A Punk Rock Family Memoir* (Touchstone, 2009), Everett True's *Hey Ho Let's Go: The Story of the Ramones* (Omnibus Press, 2002), and autobiographies by Johnny Ramone (*Commando: The Autobiography of Johnny Ramone*, Harry N. Abrams, 2012), Marky Ramone (*Punk Rock Blitzkrieg: My Life as a Ramone* with Rich Herschlag, Touchstone, 2015), Richie Ramone (*I Know Better Now: My Life Before, During, and After the Ramones* with Peter Aaron, Backbeat, 2018), and Dee Dee Ramone (*Poison*

*Heart: Surviving the Ramones* with Veronica Kofman, Helter Skelter Publishing, 1998, subsequently reissued as *Lobotomy: Surviving the Ramones*). There are more, and I'm delighted that *Gabba Gabba Hey! A Conversation with the Ramones* can join all of them on the bookshelf.

Thanks also to my *This is Rock 'n' Roll Radio* cohost Dana Bonn and my friend Dave Murray. Thanks to my mom and dad and my uncle Carl, all passed from this world, but their belief in me sustains me still. Thanks also to my brothers, Art and Rob, and to my sister, Denise. Special thanks to my daughter Meghan Jean Cafarelli for sharing her publishing expertise, and to my wife Brenda Nuremberg-Cafarelli for helping me transcribe the interviews and for believing in me. Something to believe in? I believe in miracles, 'cause I'm one.

# OVERTURE

## *The Kids Are All Hopped Up and Ready to Go*

(In 2000, a friend named Eric Strattman was soliciting contributions for a fanzine called *Angst & Daisies*. Like most writers, I'm always eager to write without actually getting paid for it, so I wrote the following in answer to the question posed to us: *What was the album that changed your life?*)

The *album* that changed my life? Oh, no—we'll have none of that in this corner! While this is certainly a popular question for this sort of exercise (a CD buyer's guide to which I contributed a few years back peppered its regular listings with sidebars consisting of the replies given by various Famous People to that very same question), I personally reject it with the specific intent of setting it afire and going wee-wee all over its smoldering embers.

It's not that I don't believe a record album can change one's life; I do believe it, and anyway, I've read too many testimonials of such conversions to ever dismiss 'em all out of hand. And besides, a record did change my life. It just wasn't an album that did the deed. It was a single, a 45-rpm single, the building block of rock 'n' roll. One sublime song on a 7-inch slab o' vinyl was all it took. Lemme tell ya 'bout it….

As a child growing up in the sixties and seventies, my musical preferences were largely shaped by AM Top 40 radio. The Beatles, of course, were inescapable; when I was four years old, I saw *A Hard Day's Night* at the local drive-in, so I'm all set whenever someone gets around to asking me about the movie that changed my life. A couple of years later, we had *The Monkees* on TV every week. We had that great, transcendent TV commercial for Radio Free Europe, wherein an Eastern European DJ used the Drifters' "On Broadway" as the living, thriving embodiment of truth, justice, and the American way, baby.

And we had the radio, pumping out an endless supply of rockin' pop, from the Rolling Stones to the Archies, Herman's Hermits, the American Breed, Gary Lewis and the Playboys, the Castaways, the Surfaris, Jefferson Airplane. We had "I Fought the Law" by the Bobby Fuller Four and "I Like It like That" by the Dave Clark Five, two songs that I only ever seemed to hear in my brother's red convertible, thus convincing me that his was the only radio that played those songs. And that's just the stuff that I specifically remember being aware of as a grade school kid.

I continued to listen faithfully to AM radio right through my freshman and sophomore years in high school, rushing on a steady barrage of short, sharp songs that just had to be played over and over again. I had favorite albums, too—if you'd asked me today's question in 1976 or '77, I'd have dutifully answered *Sgt. Pepper* or *Abbey Road*, with an honorable mention for maybe the White Album, plus the Sweet's *Desolation Boulevard*, the Monkees' *Pisces, Aquarius, Capricorn & Jones Ltd.*, even—believe it or not!—Fleetwood Mac's *Rumours*. But these were all merely records that I liked to play, alongside my regular diet of 45s and compilation LPs. There was nothing here to really change my life. Yet.

The seeds of the revolution were planted by a music tabloid called *Phonograph Record Magazine*. As a senior in high school, I picked up a couple of issues of *PRM*, which were sponsored as giveaways by WOUR-FM, the Utica, NY album-rock station that had stolen my loyalty away from the now-disco AM stations. (WOUR also played the Kinks, a band I'd recently discovered thanks to sage advice from my sister, so AM radio *really* couldn't compete like it used to.)

*PRM* seemed to me like a communiqué from another world, especially with its coverage of something called punk rock, which intrigued me endlessly. To this day, I can't explain the instant fascination I felt with this sound I'd never actually heard, and with groups I'd never heard of: Eddie and the Hot Rods. Blondie. The Sex Pistols. And, most importantly, the Ramones.

The descriptions of the Ramones captivated me. They seemed like they must be horrible, degenerate, almost criminal. They also seemed like they might be the most exciting rock 'n' roll band imaginable. I was scared of them, and I was hooked on 'em body and soul before I ever heard a note of their music.

In the summer of '77, the year I graduated from high school, I heard punk rock for the first time when WOUR played the Sex Pistols' new single, "God Save the Queen." It didn't quite change my life, but the seeds were taking root. During a vacation in Cleveland, I saw some of the records I'd been reading about but couldn't quite make the commitment to actually buy them yet. That fall, I started college in Brockport, NY, and the campus radio station finally allowed me to hear Blondie, Television, and the Ramones. I didn't immediately fall as hard for the Ramones as I thought I might, but I was still hooked. And I finally gave in and bought my first two punk rock singles. One was the import single of the Sex Pistols' "God Save the Queen," which I remembered from its spin on WOUR. The other was a Ramones record that I hadn't yet heard: "Sheena Is a Punk Rocker."

I didn't even own a stereo at the time. So, I had to wait until Thanksgiving break to actually hear my new acquisitions. Back home for the holidays, I played "God Save the Queen," and it was good. And then I played "Sheena Is a Punk Rocker" for the first time.

It played. And I stared at the record, watching it spin as it played. The record ended.

And I got up and played it again. And again. And again. And several more agains after that.

I swear to God, I suddenly felt taller. Colors seemed brighter. The confusing world of a seventeen-year-old all at once…well, nothing can make sense of a seventeen-year-old's world, but clarity seemed within reach. I had never heard anything like this record! I played it again. And I played it again.

It sounded like the Beach Boys, like the AM pop music that I always loved, and continued to love. But it was faster, fuller, innately louder even at low volume. Everything was different. Nothing was the same. My life, like Lou Reed (almost) said, was changed by rock 'n' roll.

About a month after first hearing "Sheena Is a Punk Rocker," I wrote my first essay on rock 'n' roll music, extolling the virtues of punk rock in general and the Ramones in particular. It was published as an emeritus contribution in my high school newspaper (a far cooler publication than the reactionary rag at my college, which reviewed the Sex Pistols' album by saying something to the effect that, "Put simply, this record sucks."). My essay became the focal point for the nascent punk scene at my alma mater. A few months later, *Bomp!* magazine published a special issue devoted to power pop, a label that seemed to perfectly describe the type of music I loved the most; *Bomp!* even listed "Sheena Is a Punk Rocker" as one of power pop's definitive records.

In between, in January of 1978, I saw a local punk/power pop group called the Flashcubes, and my fate was sealed. I'd found my music, and I would preach its virtues forevermore. Many factors led to this point, from the British Invasion and its aftermath in the sixties, to my vicarious fascination with punk via *Phonograph Record Magazine*. But it was "Sheena Is a Punk Rocker" that accomplished the change. And, right now, it's high time I played that record again. And again. And again.

—

In 1994, I was a frequent freelance contributor to *Goldmine* magazine, a bi-weekly tabloid produced for record collectors. *Goldmine* was edited at the time by a gentleman named Jeff Tamarkin, and in 1994, Jeff was actively looking for articles to tie in with the magazine's year-

14

long celebration of its twentieth anniversary. Since the Ramones were also hitting the twenty-year mark in '94, I pitched Jeff on the sheer inevitability of a Ramones cover story, and he agreed. Jeff contacted the Ramones' people; the group's publicist, the wonderful Ida Langsam, set me up for phone interviews with each of them: I could call Joey at this number at this time; I could not call Johnny at all, but should expect a call from him precisely at *this* time. Johnny called right on schedule; Joey wasn't even home when I called.

Disappointed that the interview was apparently not going to happen, I left a message on Joey's answering machine. Joey called me back, apologized profusely, and asked me if we could still do the interview, like, maybe an hour from now, ya know? I was delighted to comply.

(After speaking with Joey for something like two and a half hours that night, I was stunned when he called me back unexpectedly a week later. Having covered the Ramones' history in our initial conversation, Joey wanted to be sure I knew about his other current projects: a duet with General Johnson [formerly of the Chairmen of the Board] on a Southern beach music cover of "Rockaway Beach," which would be included on a compilation called *Godchildren of Soul*; a recording project with his brother, Mickey Leigh, billed as Sibling Rivalry, covering Blodwyn Pig's "See My Way"; his appearance on a songwriters' showcase compilation called *In Their Own Words*, singing "I Wanna Be Sedated" with musical support from Andy Shernoff of the Dictators; and his desire to work again with Holly Beth Vincent [ex of Holly and the Italians], with whom Joey had dueted on a cover of Sonny and Cher's "I Got You Babe" for single release back in 1982. Unprepared for the call, I didn't have a cassette ready to record the conversation, so I just scribbled notes as fast as I could. It still ranks as one of the most pleasant surprise phone calls I've ever received, to pick up the receiver and hear, "Hi, Carl? It's Joey Ramone.")

Ida was only able to set up interviews with the then-current members of the band. I also very much wanted to interview Tommy Ramone and Richie Ramone, and I was dying to get in touch with Dee Dee Ramone. But these were not to be. That said, the interviews with Joey, Johnny, Marky, and C. J. were everything I could hope they'd be. My wife Brenda helped me transcribe the hours of tapes, and then I tried to assemble them all into something resembling a conversation, creating the illusion of all four Ramones sitting and chatting together at the same time.

At the time, no one knew how unlikely that would be, to *ever* have all the Ramones together, sitting and chatting at the same time. In later years, we'd find out that Joey and Johnny hated each other, that they virtually never spoke to each other, that tension was a way of life if you were a Ramone. There are hints of that tension in these interviews, but it was still a secret and none of the brudderhood was prepared to reveal that to outsiders. Semper Fi.

I went into this project unapologetically starry-eyed. Still am, really. I had always felt that the Ramones did not get their just due, and I wanted to give them a spotlight, a cover story, a big ol' showcase for the members of the band to tell their own tale. *Goldmine*'s managing editor Bonni Miller somehow made it all fit within one single, glorious issue.

The resulting piece, "Twenty Years of 'Gabba Gabba Hey': The Few, the Proud, the Ramones," was published in the September 30, 1994, issue of *Goldmine*. Management secured permission to wrap it all up with a cartoon cover by *The Simpsons*' creator Matt Groening, depicting Homer Simpson cheering the Ramones on. I had requested that cover but didn't learn it had happened until I saw the issue on the stands. What a great, fulfilling memory.

When the Ramones were inducted into the Rock and Roll Hall of Fame in 2002, the hall's website cited my original article in its short list of "Recommended Reading" on the Ramones. (How short was the list? Three items. The list consisted of Jim Bessman's terrific book

*Ramones: An American Band*, a late seventies article from *Rolling Stone*, and my *Goldmine* piece. I'll risk the sin of pride and say that's kind of a big deal.)

Periodicals have a limited shelf life, so this material has effectively been out of print for nearly thirty years. It's time we fixed that. Hell, it's time we expanded that. What follows is not the article that appeared in *Goldmine*—I had no interest in merely reprising that—but rather a fuller representation of my interviews with some guys who shared the stage surname Ramone. It's too big a record for just a magazine. We need a whole book here.

Hey-ho…ya know?

# INTRODUCTION

## Hey-Ho, Let's Go!

The Ramones are arguably the single most influential rock 'n' roll act to emerge from that curious muddle of magic and mediocrity called the 1970s. If you think it's strange to refer to a noisy quartet of willful misfits—a group whose minimalist approach may seem to border on parody and/or simple ineptitude, a group which never had any hit records, a group which rarely received radio play outside of college stations, a group that was still waiting to break through to mass popular recognition when it finally cashed in its chips after more than twenty years of bubbling under—and if you just can't understand why anyone could consider this three-chord band of glue-sniffing punks so friggin' important, then you better sit down, kids, 'cause it's time for your history lesson right here at Rock 'n' Roll High School.

The Ramones were unlike any rock 'n' roll band the world had ever heard before. Oh, they had obvious antecedents; MC5, the Stooges, the New York Dolls, and the Dictators each provided early models of thunderous amateurism and out-for-kicks abandon. But the Ramones reinterpreted all of that—plus myriad influences encompassing Freddy "Boom Boom" Cannon, the Beach Boys, Alice Cooper, the Ohio Express, the Who, the Ronettes, and Herman's Hermits—at the garage-band level. In the process, they revved-up the tempo, stripping the music of all extraneous clutter, surrendering all waste to the exhilarating thrill of the forward thrust. The Ramones didn't just play songs; they pummeled their way through them with the piledriving determination of Sgt. Fury and his Howling Commandos moving through occupied Europe.

If you doubt the pervasiveness of the Ramones' influence on pop music, look at the top of the pops. Sure, you've never seen "I Wanna Be Sedated" or "Judy Is a Punk" in the Top 40 listings but consider the differences between some of the chart-toppers of 1974 and the popular music of 1994, when these interviews were conducted. Some things may have remained unchanged, but there's simply no way to get from "(You're) Having My Baby" and "I Honestly Love You" to "Smells Like Teen Spirit" and—God knows!—Green Day without at least considering the Ramones as a significant contributing factor.

And now? It wouldn't surprise me if you saw some random kid today, someone far too young to remember the Ramones first-hand, nonetheless sporting a Ramones T-shirt. It doesn't even matter if such kids really know the Ramones or if they just think the damned shirt looks cool. It's evidence of the Ramones' assimilation into the greater pop culture. In the seventies, they were outsiders, square pegs. Today, the Ramones are the Beatles, Bob Marley, Jimi Hendrix, the Doors, AC/DC, Nirvana, Batman. The Ramones are everywhere.

It sure is a long way from the Ramones' secret origin in 1974. What, not even fifty years ago? Man, it was a million years ago.

In 1974, four guys from Forest Hills, Queens, became the Ramones. Guitarist Johnny Cummings and drummer Tommy Erdelyi had been in a high school group called Tangerine Puppets (playing bass and guitar, respectively). Tangerine Puppets broke up while the pair were still in high school. Erdelyi went on to become a recording engineer at the Record Plant in Manhattan, where he would work on Jimi Hendrix's *Band of Gypsys* album, and on records by Mountain and John McLaughlin.

Meanwhile, Cummings had formed his new band with two neighbors, Douglas Colvin on bass and vocals, and lanky Jeffrey Hyman on drums. Hyman had sung for a glitter band called Sniper, and soon moved from the drum seat to the lead vocal spot in this new group. Erdelyi expressed interest in becoming the group's manager; frustration with the fruitless search for an appropriately minimalist drummer led him to occupy the drum spot himself, even though he had never drummed before. A fifth member, identified only as Ritchie, was in and out of the group in the blink of an eye.

The group gelled—primitive, amateur, and untrained, but possessed of an unmatched adrenaline buzz. There remained one final rite of passage. Seeking a group identity, the band members discarded their surnames in favor of a uniform *nom du guerre*, inspired by a pseudonym once used by Paul McCartney. Johnny Cummings, Jeffrey Hyman, Tommy Erdelyi, and Douglas Colvin ceased to exist; in their place were Johnny, Joey, Tommy, and Dee Dee Ramone. The Ramones had been born, and there was nothing anyone could do about it.

They were far from an immediate hit. Audiences didn't know what to make of this loud, bizarre group. But the Ramones persevered. They got tighter and, of course, *faster!* They began playing at a filthy Bowery club called CBGB's and developed a following. Word of mouth spread, and an unlikely scene began to develop at both CBGB's and another club, Max's Kansas City—a scene centered around the varied talents of groups like the Heartbreakers (featuring former New York Dolls Johnny Thunders and Jerry Nolan), Blondie, Talking Heads, Richard Hell and the Voidoids, and Television. Somebody applied the name "punk" to the scene, recalling cantankerous sixties groups like the Standells and the Shadows of Knight. No band embodied that scene quite like the Ramones did.

The Ramones acquired a manager, former MC5 publicist and *16 Magazine* coeditor, Danny Fields. The group signed a record deal with Sire Records, an independent record company run by the near-visionary Seymour Stein. Their first album, *Ramones*, was released in 1976.

The galvanizing "Hey-ho, let's go!" chant of "Blitzkrieg Bop" kicked off *Ramones*, a record that was raw, jarring, and much, much more primal than the polished sounds of the day. Song titles like "Now I Wanna Sniff Some Glue" and "Today Your Love, Tomorrow the World" conveyed a cartoon depravity, and the Ramones reveled in their own fascination with American junk culture, from B-grade horror films to fast food and 7-11s.

*Ramones* also displayed the group's own bizarre Top 40/bubblegum aspirations, as the almost-jangly (sort of) "I Wanna Be Your Boyfriend" and a cover of Chris Montez's "Let's Dance" reflected undisguised pop sensibilities. The album may not have seemed like a professional product by the slick standards of radio, but it was a revelation nonetheless.

The Ramones toured and played constantly. A visit to England in 1976 provided impetus for the British punk movement, as various working-class zeroes (many already in bands or in the act of forming bands, and some not even to that embryonic step) were suddenly inspired by the Ramones: the Sex Pistols, the Clash, the Damned, the Buzzcocks, the Adverts, and virtually every other name in the first wave of British punk. This reaction was not confined to the United Kingdom. In the 1990 video *Lifestyles of the Ramones*, Sire's Howie Klein would look back on the Ramones as "the Johnny Appleseeds of the whole New Wave movement:" they would play somewhere, and within weeks new bands would sprout.

The 1977 *Leave Home* album had a fuller sound, courtesy of coproducer Tommy. The chainsaw buzz of the first album gave way to a slightly purer pop approach, but thematic concerns remained largely unchanged in songs like "Gimme Gimme Shock Treatment" and "You're Gonna Kill That Girl." "Pinhead" offered another sloganeering shout-along in the "Blitzkrieg Bop" tradition, its "Gabba Gabba Hey!" refrain inspired by a line in the 1932 horror film *Freaks*. "Carbona Not Glue," the logical sequel to "Now I Wanna Sniff Some Glue," appeared on initial pressings of *Leave Home*, but was removed from later pressings when the manufacturers of Carbona Spot Remover threatened legal action. (Lousy corporate weasels!)

A non-LP single, "Sheena Is a Punk Rocker," provided the Ramones with their first brush of pop immortality, as it became the first punk or new wave single to break into *Billboard*'s Hot 100 singles chart. It subsequently replaced "Carbona Not Glue" on domestic copies of *Leave Home*; a then-unreleased song called "Babysitter" replaced "Carbona Not Glue" on the British version of *Leave Home*.

"Sheena" also turned up, remixed, as an album track on *Rocket to Russia*, perhaps the definitive Ramones album and one of the greatest blasts of rockin' pop imaginable. The "Rockaway Beach" single likewise breached the Hot 100, but a terrific cover of the Bobby Freeman/Beach Boys staple "Do You Wanna Dance" stiffed, effectively ending the Ramones' Top 40 hopes.

Tired of life on the road, Tommy retired from the band in 1978, though he remained involved as a producer. His replacement was Marc Bell (henceforth Marky Ramone), formerly of the group Dust and then a member of Richard Hell and the Voidoids. The subsequent *Road to Ruin* album seemed to find the Ramones in darker spirits, with the warped sun 'n' fun illusions of the previous album replaced by a despondent gloom typified by tracks like "I Wanted Everything." It was a much heavier sounding record than the first three, but it was no less memorable. And it contained "I Wanna Be Sedated," which would become one of the Ramones' all-time best-known recordings.

Meanwhile, a live gig (with Tommy) in London on New Year's Eve, 1977, was preserved on *It's Alive!*, a furious double-LP set that Sire, maddeningly, refused to issue in the United States. Bastards! In between albums and tours, the Ramones appeared in New World Pictures' *Rock 'n' Roll High School*, a 1979 drive-in ode to teen rebellion, produced by B-movie kingpin Roger Corman and directed by Allan Arkush. The group teamed with legendary record producer Phil Spector for 1980's *End of the Century* album. Spector's elaborate production techniques and sometimes abrasive personality (How's *that* for an understatement?) frequently clashed with the Ramones' straight-ahead style. Things got even glossier with 1981's *Pleasant Dreams*, produced by 10cc's Graham Gouldman. By this time, the

Ramones had split with Danny Fields and were now managed by Gary Kurfirst. Kurfirst would remain the group's manager for the remainder of their career.

The 1983 *Subterranean Jungle* album returned the Ramones to more familiar bubblepunk terrain, but it was also the first Ramones album to be deleted from the catalog by Sire. Marky's battle with alcoholism prompted him to leave the band following the album's release. He was replaced by Richie Reinhardt, a.k.a. Richie Beau, a.k.a. Richie Ramone.

The *Too Tough to Die* album in 1984 found the Ramones reclaiming their hard-rock crown, venturing closer to heavy metal territory and even presenting two tracks ("Wart Hog" and "Endless Vacation") of eighties-style hardcore from the band that inspired that whole genre. "Bonzo Goes to Bitburg," a 1985 European single, offered a devastating anti-Reagan rant, somewhat jarring when coming from a band heretofore more associated with an implicit right-wing world view.

"Bonzo Goes to Bitburg" was retitled "My Brain Is Hanging Upside Down" by the time it appeared on the 1986 *Animal Boy* album, a record that also contained the seemingly radio-ready tune "Something to Believe In"; in spite of an endorsement from *Billboard* and an amusingly snarky video for "Something to Believe In," radio apparently still wasn't quite ready to believe, and a hit record once again eluded the Ramones. The 1987 *Halfway to Sanity* album was highlighted by the near-psychedelic "Garden of Serenity" and the chillingly uplifting "I Wanna Live," plus guest vocals by Debbie Harry on "Go Lil' Camaro Go."

Richie left the band suddenly over a salary dispute in 1987. Following a pair of disastrous gigs with ex-Blondie drummer Clem Burke (who reportedly wanted to be billed as "Elvis Ramone" if he'd stayed with the band), a now clean and sober Marky Ramone returned to the Ramones. Marky remained a Ramone until the group's demise.

In 1989, the Ramones provided the title tune to the film version of Stephen King's *Pet Sematary*. That track was included on the *Brain Drain* album, as was "I Believe in Miracles," a stunning affirmation of faith in the face of adversity with its ruggedly determined optimism sufficient to give even the most jaded cynics gooseflesh.

So, it was a shock when "I Believe in Miracles" author Dee Dee Ramone abruptly—*very* abruptly—left the Ramones in 1989. As Dee Dee King, Dee Dee had already released a rap single, "Funky Man," and an album called *Standing in the Spotlight*. Although the group had changed drummers a few times, they'd never had to face the loss of such a key member and songwriter. By any reasonable expectation, Dee Dee's departure should have been the end of the Ramones.

But these guys were too tough to die, remember? Auditions brought in Christopher Ward, rechristened as C. J. Ramone. C. J., a mere lad of twenty-four when he joined the group, was AWOL from the Marines at the time. He spent three weeks in the brig before being granted a discharge, freeing him to take on bass duties with the few, the proud, the Ramones.

The CD boom prompted the reissue of now-classic early Ramones tracks. Sire had released a best-of set, *Ramones Mania*, in 1988. In 1990, it was joined by *All the Stuff (And More), Volume One*, a single CD combining *Ramones* and *Leave Home* (minus "Carbona Not Glue"), plus some bonus live and demo tracks. A second volume appeared in 1991, exhuming *Rocket to Russia* and *Road to Ruin*. The remaining studio albums in the catalogue were reissued individually in 1994, and the first four were eventually also reissued as separate CDs. Even *It's Alive!* was finally released on CD in 1995, that live album's looooong-overdue American debut.

The Ramones bid a fond farewell to Sire Records with—wait for it!—a live album, *Loco Live*, in 1992. Though nowhere near the same caliber as *It's Alive!*, *Loco Live* did include a live (and unlisted) "Carbona Not Glue" as a going-away present. So long, Seymour.

The group signed with Radioactive, a new label run by the Ramones' manager, Gary Kurfirst. Their first album for the label, *Mondo Bizarro*, was released in 1992, and it included three new tracks written by Dee Dee. An album of sixties covers, *Acid Eaters*, was released in 1994.

The Ramones celebrated their 20th anniversary in 1994. These interviews with Joey, Johnny, Marky, and C. J. Ramone were conducted in commemoration of that anniversary. Although the Ramones had never enjoyed the popular success they deserved, by 1994 they had become an increasingly prominent reference point for more and more artists. Acts as diverse as the Human League and Motörhead, Chris Isaak and Nirvana, had acknowledged their debt to and/or admiration for the Ramones. The Ramones had finally gotten that ever-elusive gold record, as *Ramones Mania* was certified gold that spring. They even appeared on *The Simpsons* television show, an unassailable sign of forbiddingly cool status.

After twenty years and over 2,000 performances, the time was drawing near when the Ramones would finally hang up their leather jackets for good. They would begin recording their final studio album, 1995's *¡Adios Amigos!*, later that year; they would play their final live show in Los Angeles on August 6, 1996. They would never reunite. By definition, a road to ruin has to end sometime.

But in 1994, that road had not quite ended yet. My conversations with the Ramones follows as each of the then-current members took the opportunity to look back and to comment at length on the group's history. Then, as now, the interviews reinforce a long-held belief that this was a band that was never in it for the perceived glory. The Ramones' commitment to the band was evident in Marky's reminiscences of his first exposure to the group, in Joey's calling this writer back a week after the interview because he'd thought of some additional comments he had wanted to make, in C. J.'s palpable thrill just at being in this band he'd admired for years, and in Johnny's sincere curiosity regarding what the interviewer thought of each Ramones album.

There have been many great bands in rock 'n' roll history, but only a handful can be recognized instantly just by their first names. You know John, Paul, George, and Ringo. Ladies and gentlemen, here's Johnny, Joey, Marky, and C. J.—the Ramones!

1-2-3-4!

# GABBA GABBA HEY!

## A Conversation with the Ramones

*We're going to go through a verbal discography of the Ramones' career, an album-by-album discussion and a couple of miscellaneous tracks thrown in here and there. Let's start with the origins of the Ramones and the early demos you did—your memories of those.*

**JOHNNY:** Okay.

*How did those demo tracks come to be done?*

**JOEY:** I guess the first demo that we had done was a fifteen-song demo that we did somewhere out in Long Island. Tommy knew a studio, and he produced it. And we each put up a thousand dollars to pay for it. And it came out really good. Tommy thinks it's more, maybe, arty to some degree, you know what I mean?

**JOHNNY:** I'm not sure when we did it. Let me see, probably late in '74? We did them all in one day, mixing and playing.

*I think it was either Johnny or Dee Dee who said the demo came out better than the first album did. Does that sound right?*

**JOHNNY:** The demo came out fine. I don't know if it's better in any way [than the first Ramones album]. It came out fine.

**JOEY:** I remember when I got my copy. In those days, it was pre-cassette, and I had my copy put on to an eight-track cartridge.

And I remember I gave it to my brother's wife for safekeeping, and that was the last I saw of it. I think I maybe heard it once or twice.

I remember when we would send them around, we'd get it back with maybe thirty seconds of the tape being played. I mean, those were the days of Led Zeppelin and the likes of people like that. And the kind of music that we were playing was pretty alien, you know? Pretty foreign to the days of Foreigner and Kansas and all that stuff.

*Almost like shock treatment.*

**JOEY:** Yeah, like shock treatment.

*Is any of that stuff ever likely to see the light of day?*

**JOEY:** I know Tommy still has the master. And on *All the Stuff (And More), Volume One* we put, I think, three tracks on from that tape. We put on "I Can't Be," and then there was a song called "I Don't Wanna Be Learned/I Don't Wanna Be Tamed."

*Subsequently, you recorded two tracks for Marty Thau, who had managed the New York Dolls.*

**JOHNNY:** Oh, boy! Yeah, "I Wanna Be Your Boyfriend" and "Judy Is a Punk."

**JOEY:** Yeah, we hooked up. Marty wanted to get together with us and he wanted to produce us. We did two tracks with him that appeared on that *Groups of Wrath* [a various artists compilation CD released in 1991]. Actually, I thought those versions came out great. I thought "Boyfriend" came out much better than the Sire version, you know; I thought it was a much better version. And I remember "Judy Is a Punk," he put a piano on it, which, I don't know, sounds kinda weird.

But that was after the Dolls, and he wanted to manage us and produce us. And we didn't want him managing us. [But] we took a shot, ya know? I mean, we did it free and the whole bit. He covered the expenses. We did it up by his house, in those days before he lost it [laughs]. Actually, it was a good experience.

**JOHNNY:** I think Marty was looking to be the producer or something. [But] Tommy wanted to be the producer, Tommy Ramone. We were really looking more for a manager. So, [Tommy] was a little reluctant to be working with Marty or to go any further along with that.

*How did you get from those demos to a contract with Sire?*

**JOHNNY:** We picked a few songs off the demo tape, and we started sending them out to record companies. [Veteran songwriter and producer] Richard Gottehrer came down to our rehearsal, wanted to see us, and was interested in doing a single of "You're Gonna Kill That Girl." We weren't looking for any single deal, so we said, "No, we're not interested." We wanted an album deal. We weren't looking to be on any of these compilations of other bands, like the CBGB's or Max's stuff or anything. We were just looking for a straight album deal.

**JOEY:** I think initially they wanted to do a single with us, and we were holding out for an album.

I remember back at that period, the days of CBGB's, I guess we were doing well. And I guess when there was that CBGB festival that we had won the first night, and press was there from all over the world, *Rolling Stone* and *NME*—I mean, that just really kind of capped it for us. After that night, we kind of stole the show.

But I guess around that period there would be a lot of different labels comin' around. Like, I remember Clive Davis would come down, and he'd say, "They're great, but they'll never get it down on wax." And Elektra/Asylum was interested, and Sire was interested.

And we went with Sire because we didn't want to get lost in the shuffle of a major label. At the time, Sire was an independent company. And we felt that Seymour [Stein, president of Sire] understood what we were about. So, we went with Sire.

*Your debut album,* Ramones, *was recorded very quickly.*

**JOEY:** Yeah, it was around a week [laughs]. We did it down in the bowels of Radio City Music Hall. Yeah, we did it pretty quick.

**JOHNNY:** It was recorded fairly quickly. We had to do something over, I don't know what it was, but we had to go back and do a day's work over or something. We did it in some studio that was in Radio City Music Hall, I believe.

Basically, we'd do a take, and they would talk to me and say, "Well, you wanna come in here and listen to it?" I'd go, "Why? Was it good?" And they'd go, "Yeah, it's fine. Do you just wanna hear it?" And I'd go, "No, forget it, let's go to the next song."

I think I went through like six songs in a row like that, without going and listening to any of them. I figured, "All right, they say it's fine. Why waste time going back and listening to it?" I still don't even like doing that. I still don't even like going back in. If it's fine, why can't we just do the next song [laughs]?

**JOEY:** Tommy and Craig Leon coproduced together. And actually, when Tommy joined the band, initially he was advising us, and we were trying to find a drummer who was more simplistic. And in those days, everybody was very flashy, very show-offish. So, eventually we just said, "Tommy, why don't you play the drums?"

Tommy was a producer. He had worked on Jimi Hendrix's *Electric Ladyland* album, and the Mahavishnu Orchestra, I think he was involved with that. And he was a guitar player. So, it was kind of funny how things wound up.

*Kind of a Renaissance Ramone.*

**JOEY:** Yeah! It's funny because everybody adapted Tommy's drum style. You know, like Paul Cook [of the Sex Pistols], and people of that nature. It's pretty ironic, ya know?

JOHNNY: We played a little slow then. Maybe at the time it might seem fast, but now that I listen back, we weren't going too fast at that point. We got a little [faster] by the first album, but to me it still sounds like it drags a bit. About the second or third album, it started sounding about right.

*To achieve that level of Ramones velocity.*

JOHNNY: Yeah. You know everyone thought we were playing very fast, but now it needs to be stepped up a little bit.

JOEY: So, we did that album, I think we did it in about a week. I remember we mixed it in a night. And I remember one night during the mix, we were working on "Blitzkrieg Bop," and [album producer] Craig Leon started telling us a story about a Ouija board. And he was telling us the first time he ever tried a Ouija board, it spelled out "devil." And then the song just, like, *disappeared*! Like it was erased or something. "Blitzkrieg Bop." It was real weird.

*It's that Satanic music stuff.*

JOEY: [laughs]

*See, Tipper Gore was right about you guys!*

JOEY: It was very freaky, ya know?

*Except for the cover of Chris Montez's "Let's Dance," all of the songwriting was credited to the whole group. How did the songwriting chores actually break down? Did everyone contribute?*

JOHNNY: Slightly. We just wanted to keep it that way. Different people wrote different songs on the first [album]. On all the albums, different people had written songs, it wasn't really group efforts. Couple of songs might have been a group effort, but we each had our own songs.

JOEY: Well, I guess in the earliest days, we wanted the band kind of seen as a unit, kind of a union of sorts. But basically, it was me and Dee Dee who were the chief songwriters. Though the band contributed as a whole on a bunch of the songs.

But, just to name a few of the songs, like, Tommy had written "I Wanna Be Your Boyfriend"; that was, I think, one of the only songs he'd written with us. And "Blitzkrieg Bop" was Dee Dee, and "Judy Is a Punk" and "Beat on the Brat" was me. The songs about Germany were Dee Dee, you know, those war-type songs. Because Dee Dee's roots were back in Germany, he was kind of a war brat. He had that kind of fascination, ya know? And then John and Dee Dee wrote "I Don't Wanna Go Down in the Basement" and "Loudmouth."

JOHNNY: We just left it [as a group credit]. I had always liked it better that way. I had seen other bands, I think the Doors [took a group credit], and I always thought that was nice.

*A group identity.*

JOHNNY: A group identity, get away from the individualism and maybe keep your ego more in check.

JOEY: I mean, it was really kind of playing together, but me and Dee Dee were....

*The principal songwriters?*

JOEY: Yeah, we had our own approach. I mean, it all worked out nice.

*What were the influences in creating the Ramones' sound? Did you have conscious models in mind?*

JOEY: Oh yeah, there were thousands of influences. We were all rock 'n' roll fans right from the start. I mean, we were all big record collectors and fans and this and that. But the songs [we wrote], you know, the influences were, I mean, thousands and thousands of influences from the inception of rock 'n' roll. From Elvis Presley, Buddy Holly, and through the sixties.

I mean, the sixties to me was the most influential time in the history of rock 'n' roll music. There were so many different styles, things that went down. The fifties were the infancy, and the sixties were, you know, very influential and very more experimental. And then, by the seventies in England, I guess, with the glitter thing for the most part. And in the late sixties, the Stooges and MC5, and [in the seventies] Slade and T. Rex and Alice Cooper and all that stuff. But yeah, I guess all that. I mean, I know we always stayed real open-minded.

**JOHNNY:** We started off, and I think we wanted to be a bubblegum band. At one point, the Bay City Rollers were becoming popular. They had written "Saturday Night," and we then sat down and said, "We have to write a song with a chant in it, like they have." So, we wrote "Blitzkrieg Bop." Somehow, in our warped minds, I think we thought we were a bubblegum group.

*You weren't that far off, that's the thing that's amazing. I think a lot of us had to have it pointed out to us, but it's really not that far of a jump from the Bay City Rollers to the Ramones.*

**JOHNNY:** And that's what we were doing. Some of the songs I had written were not as poppy, they'd be more of the punk ones. And Dee Dee was always kind of crazy. Like on the first album, he'd written "Today Your Love, Tomorrow the World" and "53rd & 3rd." They're not really bubblegum songs.

**JOEY:** And, ya know, it was about music but it was about everything. As far as where different ideas came from, it was really just from personal experience, and from film and TV and relationships and just life, ya know? Just kind of adventuring and experiencing different situations.

**JOHNNY:** I think I was just learning how to play. I had never played, so it wasn't a question of being influenced by somebody else, where you sit there and learn how to play their riffs or anything like that. I just started from scratch here, and we tried to play what we were capable of and write what we were capable of playing.

**JOEY:** Also, on the first album, we tried to create kind of a situation where it was vocals and drums on one side and [guitar on the other]. We tried something, but it was more experimental.

**JOHNNY:** Well, the first time we split the stuff, [it] probably didn't really work. That's probably why nobody really does it. We probably had some good idea, because the Beatles were sort of splitting. They were splitting vocals on one side and music on the other. So, we thought, well, bass guitars on one side and guitars on the other side. [But] it sort of dilutes it.

*What are your memories of* Leave Home, *featuring the great lost Ramones track, "Carbona Not Glue"?*

**JOEY:** I think that was around the period where we started going on the road for long periods of time. Because I guess in the earliest days, when the first album came out, we would play Boston a lot because it was very liberal and open-minded. And we played Toronto a lot because it was very open as well. And New York. But we didn't really venture too far.

[But] I guess the first album, though, we had done our first cross-country tour. And all the labels kind of watched our progress before they would sign everybody else. And I remember playing Texas, with disco balls in the ceiling and the whole bit. So, by *Leave Home*, we would be touring constantly. We would be working pretty much 365 days a year. I mean, Danny [Fields] really had us working, ya know?

**JOHNNY:** Three different versions of [*Leave Home*], one with "Babysitter," another with "Sheena," between the English and

American versions. Tony Bongiovi did it, right? Yeah, he was pretty much doing the work at that point. I think the next album, the third album, he got credit for producing it, but I don't remember him being hardly even there. It was Ed Stasium doing it at that point. Ed was the engineer on *Leave Home*.

**JOEY:** The second album, we worked with Tony Bongiovi, and Ed Stasium came in as engineer, and that was when we first hooked up with Ed. And I think the second album was really powerful and punchy, much more exciting, ya know—my personal opinion.

**JOHNNY:** I don't really remember much about [recording] it. I like the album. I mean, it's one of my favorites. I think *Rocket to Russia* is my favorite, and that might be my third favorite, *Leave Home*.

By the time we did the first album, we had basically most of the stuff written for the first three albums. I thought that we should record it in basically the order we had written the songs in, so that the second album would have a slight progression off the first album, so there'd be a slight difference. And the same with the third album. So, we recorded them in the order that we wrote them in.

**JOEY:** We wanted to record it in chronological order, so we did it that way. And then on *Leave Home*, actually, "Glad to See You Go" was the first song I had written with Dee Dee. I wrote the music, and he wrote the words, and it was really exciting. I remember he went out to cop dope, and when he got back, I had the music all written [laughs]. We were living together at the time.

Yeah, the songs were great. I thought it was a real strong record. And also, with "Carbona Not Glue," it was, I guess, the natural follow-up to "Now I Wanna Sniff Some Glue" [laughs]. It was a natural progression. John and Dee Dee used to like to sniff glue on the rooftops for kicks, and they tried Carbona as well. And when we wrote that song—we wrote that song all together—we thought [Carbona Spot Remover] was just a substance. We didn't realize that it was a trademark, a company name.

So, I guess Carbona threatened to sue Sire because they didn't want people to know they could get high sniffing their product. It's kind of a shame that we had to pull it, but they didn't want a lawsuit, so it was pulled. And I think it was replaced with "Sheena."

*Right, in the US it was replaced by "Sheena," and I read someplace that it was replaced by "Babysitter" in the UK.*

**JOEY:** It was "Babysitter" in England. Well, "Sheena" I had written, and actually that version [added to *Leave Home*] was more of a, I guess, AM kind of production.

*"Sheena Is a Punk Rocker" became the first punk or new wave single to dent the Billboard Hot 100 chart.*

**JOEY:** Yeah, it reached…I think it got up to about number 48. [**NOTE:** *This chart position is also cited by Jim Bessman in the book* Ramones: An American Band, *but the single actually peaked at #81 in* Billboard.] And also, it introduced surf music in conjunction with punk [laughs], punk rock. [Surf] was a real influence. And also, the lyrics really dealt with this girl [who] was leaving the old for the new at that point. And references to Sheena [*Sheena, Queen of the Jungle,* a popular 1940s comic book character, played on TV in the fifties by actress Irish McCalla] because of the primal-ness of the sound.

Actually, I remember when I wrote it. I wrote it in, um, I guess it was '76 or early '77. I remember I played it for Seymour and he freaked out. He said, "We gotta go and record this!" And we went in and recorded it right away, like, within the next night or somethin', at Sundragon, which was a really cool studio in Manhattan. I don't remember what street it was on. It was very exciting because we went in, did it, and they put it out, I guess kinda like it was in the fifties.

I guess the radio, there was a problem about [the line], "The kids are all hopped up." There was a problem about, "Can't you change 'hop' to something else?" I mean, I thought that was totally absurd, ya know? 'Cause it's an old jazz expression that I thought was cool to use.

**JOHNNY:** I don't really remember being optimistic about that yet, at that point. I think by the third album, I was getting to be a little bit more optimistic at that point. It was starting to be a movement; I felt that we sort of needed a movement. When you started seeing the Sex Pistols, Clash, all these other bands start popping up, we thought this was the right time at that point for everyone to break through and become big.

It's hard to really remember what the feeling was. "Sheena" was a hit in England, but that was never no big deal, really, having a hit in England. All that mattered, really, was America. It's okay having a hit in England, but the main thing was you wanna make it at home.

**JOEY:** Well, it would have been a hit. I didn't write it to have a hit, I wrote it because that's how I write. And it was doing really good. We were on our way to LA to do, I think, our first LA tour, California tour. And we were gonna be playing on a flatbed truck in some shopping mall with [laughs] Captain and Tennille.

And it was around that time like on *60 Minutes* when that whole thing happened with [Sex Pistols manager] Malcolm McLaren and the chains and the safety pins and the strangling each other and the crazy hair. And I guess people kinda freaked out. The hierarchy of media and the club owners and radio people and everyone kinda flipped out about it and expected the worst.

And we got kind of lumped in with [that]. Because they were looking at it as a negative, ya know, the Sex Pistols and all of what they thought goes on. It was all hype and sensationalism. So, it kinda fucked us at the same time. It kinda destroyed things.

I mean, the Sex Pistols were a great band and all, but at the same time the English bands were into this negative thing, ya know, "Destroy!" Whereas the Ramones were into a positive thing. We wanted to kind of save rock 'n' roll, keep it exciting and fun and the whole bit. Because [when] we started, the music of the day was "Disco Duck" and "Don't Rock the Boat, Baby" and Donna Summer and Kansas and Journey and Toto and REO Speedwagon—all that excitement, ya know?

*Your ambition to save rock 'n' roll culminated in* Rocket to Russia, *certainly a very positive-sounding record. Even with songs about suicides and lobotomies....*

**JOHNNY:** [laughs] That's the thing, you have to sing these things with a happy tune [laughs]!

Rocket to Russia *has been referred to as your last great commercial-sounding record, almost like the Ramones' last grand attempt at a Top 40 record.*

**JOHNNY:** That's my favorite album. It's got more classic Ramones songs on it than any other album.

**JOEY:** Well, we were never trying for anything. I mean, we did what felt right to us and was exciting to us. We never consciously tried to make a commercial record. Later on, Sire would kind of push us into working with certain producers that we didn't particularly want to work with.

**JOHNNY:** See, charts are such bullshit that I just really never took much meaning in them. It was easy for them to manipulate the charts, and I had seen those other artists and everything. You might be in the *Billboard* Top 100, but you're not in the other chart. So, how is this real? Or somebody might be in *Cashbox* or—what was the other one?—*Record World* charts, but not on the *Billboard* one. You know, charts are kinda fishy. Probably a lot of corruption goes on.

**JOEY:** So, within the same year as *Leave Home*, we put out *Rocket to Russia*. And everybody said that was our *Sgt. Pepper* [laughs], if you will. It really spoke for the whole thing, you know what I mean?

*I can't think of a single album that really sums up the whole idea of punk, new wave, even power pop, better than* Rocket to Russia *does. That is, I think, the definitive album of that style.*

**JOEY:** I mean, I guess "Blitzkrieg Bop" was a call to arms when we went over to England in '76 on July 4th, and it was kind of a call to arms for all the bands to form and the whole bit. But *Rocket to Russia*! Like, I remember one night I was hangin' out at Paul's Lounge down on Ninth Street. I ran into [guitarist/producer] Chris Spedding. Chris told me that—'cause he did the demos with [the Sex Pistols]—when he went into the studio, I think Sid or Johnny, under his arm was a copy of *Rocket to Russia*. And he said, "I wanna sound like this." Actually, it was pretty weird. Because I remember back in those days hearin' that Chris Spedding was a real nasty guy. [But] he was a nice guy, a real nice guy, and the fact that he even told me this story was pretty wild.

[**NOTE:** *Given the chronology of when Spedding worked with the Sex Pistols, the Ramones LP under whichever Pistol's arm must have been the debut album,* Ramones. *Spedding is on record as saying the Pistols' demos sounded better than the Ramones anyway. We'll agree to disagree on that point. But I also met Spedding once and will also agree that he seemed like a very nice guy.*]

*I read somewhere that no less an authority than Dr. Demento called "Teenage Lobotomy" the funniest song ever written.*

**JOHNNY:** [laughs]

**JOEY:** Yeah, I read that, too.
    "Teenage Lobotomy" kinda conjured up, ya know, being a misfit and outcast. I mean, I guess a lot of the original songs were about the feelings of alienation, frustration, ya know, being an individual. Like isolation and all of that crap, getting out your aggressions and all of that.

*Yet the cover songs on each of the Ramones' first three albums—
"Let's Dance," "California Sun," "Do You Wanna Dance," and
"Surfin' Bird"—are all real surf and sun, fun-in-the-sun tunes.*

**JOHNNY:** Yeah, yeah. We liked that we were an American band.
We generally tried to stick toward, whenever possible, American
covers. So, yeah, we were going back to basically the very early sixties
to pick songs, which was probably our first real introduction to rock
'n' roll. I mean, I was following it from the time of, say, Elvis in 1956,
but on a group thing it would probably be very early sixties.

**JOEY:** Yeah. Well, this was a time where if you supposedly weren't
serious, then you weren't a true artist. I mean, rock 'n' roll to us has
always been about fun and spirit, guts and challenge, and excitement
and raw emotional energy. And all those elements were no longer a
part of rock 'n' roll any more.

Ya know, rock 'n' roll was really washed up by the end of the
sixties. People lost sight of what it was all about, and at that point
it was all, ya know, Emerson, Lake and Palmer, Pink Floyd, and all
these people who just lost sight of [what] rock 'n' roll was about.
It was simple, ya know? I mean, the most memorable songs were
three minutes, whether it be the Beatles or the Stones or the Kinks or
the Who or whomever.

Like, when we started out, we were playing kind of simple music.
But some people referred to us as being stupid because [of what] we
were playing. I mean, the music that we grew up on was three chords.
Whether it be Little Richard or Eddie Cochran or Gene Vincent, the
best people were playing simple music that was the most memorable.

*The* Rocket to Russia *album track "Here Today, Gone Tomorrow"
actually predates the band, doesn't it?*

**JOEY:** Yeah, I had written two songs before I joined the band.
I had written "I Don't Care" and "Here Today, Gone Tomorrow."
Yeah, I mean, aside from the songwriting and all, what really made

the band special was what each band member brought to the band. Ya know, John brought a distinct guitar style, which was totally new and that was John. We each brought something totally individual, and just the chemistry—it clicked, you know what I mean? I mean, there was so much to what the Ramones were and are, you know, the whole basis for what the Ramones are—the character, the attitude, and the whole bit.

*This ties in to what you're saying. It occurs to me that the Ramones may be the last band that people identify individually, whatever the band line-up is, whether it's Dee Dee or C. J., whether it's Tommy or Marky, or Richie or Marky again. The Ramones are probably the last band, and probably the only band since the days of the Beatles and the Monkees, where people just identify them as individuals, by the first names, by just Joey-Johnny-Dee Dee-Tommy, or Joey-Johnny-C.J.-Marky.*

**JOHNNY:** [laughs]

*You, the Beatles, and the Monkees are probably the only three groups that you can say that about, just say the first names and everybody knows who you're referring to.*

**JOHNNY:** Okay.

**JOEY:** Right. Well, the last name was, ya know, a sense of unity, and the first names kept us unique individuals, which we are, and what brings the whole thing together is that everybody is a unique entity within the whole thing. Also, back in those days, music was pretty faceless.

*My point exactly. No one could ever accuse the Ramones of being faceless.*

**JOEY:** You know, of all the elements that made rock 'n' roll great, we absorbed them and they are us, or were us and are us. To me, rock 'n' roll has always been kind of coagulated, in your soul and in your blood. It's kind of a life force, ya know. It's not like, "Oh, let's be hip and form a rock 'n' roll band." It's always been kind of a part of me, as far as the whole thing.

*At this point, Tommy leaves the group.*

**JOHNNY:** He couldn't take touring, basically. There was no problem at all within the band or anything. He just could not take touring anymore. He said, "We could find a real drummer, someone who's good, and I'll show him how to play the things I've been playing."

He just felt he was having a breakdown from touring. He never felt comfortable around any sort of crowds or anything. You have to be able to deal with that kind of stuff.

**JOEY:** He couldn't handle the touring schedule anymore. It was real intense, real grueling, and he wanted to just produce. He wanted to still be involved, but he wanted to be our producer, basically.

*Is he still involved with the Ramones today?*

**JOEY:** No. We see Tommy once in a while. When we play New York, he'll come out to see us. I guess the last album he was really involved with was *Too Tough to Die*. That was a great record. But we don't see much of Tommy these days.

*Exit Tommy, enter Marky. How did you settle on Marky as Tommy's replacement?*

**JOEY:** I guess it was John who thought of Marc. And at that point, Marc was playing with Richard Hell and the Voidoids. And we kind of swiped him [laughs].

**JOHNNY:** I think he was a good drummer. We were familiar with him already from the time of Dust, even before the Ramones. He was in Richard Hell's band, and they were kind of jazzy, I thought. And I thought he was kind of wasted in that band, that he was more of a rock drummer. He looked right, he was from New York, he wore a leather jacket already—I figured that was a requirement [laughs]. Didn't have to tamper with his image or anything.

*He was born a Ramone.*

**JOHNNY:** Yeah. So, we just thought he was the best choice.

**JOEY:** I think it worked out in his best interest anyway. 'Cause Marc was always a real hard rocker. I mean, he can play anything, but he was more of a hard rock drummer. I guess he was a heavier drummer initially, and Tommy kind of showed him how to ease off of certain things. I guess he kind of combined styles.

*Marky, you recorded with Dust and with Richard Hell and the Voidoids before joining the Ramones. Was Dust your first band?*

**MARKY:** Yeah, that was in high school. I was sixteen years old when I did the first album, and I think I was in tenth grade at Erasmus High School on Flatbush Avenue in Brooklyn. And the other two guys I grew up with; the guitar player's name is Richie Wise, and the bass player's name is Kenny Aaronson. We put out two albums on Buddah Records, which was a subsidiary of Kama Sutra, which was run by Neil Bogart. We toured with Alice Cooper and Ike and Tina Turner at the time, and Uriah Heep and a lot of different bands.

But still, we were only 16 years old, and the group disbanded after two albums. That, I guess, was right after I graduated or got out of high school at the age of 18. So, Kenny decided to join Stories, of "Brother Louie" [fame], and had a hit for, I think, two weeks; it was number one in the summer of '73. The guitar player went on to produce KISS, the first two albums, *KISS* and *Hotter than Hell.*

After that, I did studio work for Andrew Oldham for Columbia Records, with a band called Estus. I was with that band for, I think, four months. I was really just there to do an album with them. And then I decided to play with Wayne County and the Backstreet Boys [on] this song "Max's Kansas City." And then I joined Richard Hell and the Voidoids. And then I joined the Ramones.

*How did you first become aware of the Ramones?*

**MARKY:** Well, I hung out at CBGB's and Max's Kansas City, and I knew Dee Dee very well. If I wasn't sitting at a table with Dee Dee or Johnny Thunders or Jerry Nolan, I'd be at a table with, let's see, who else? So many people around in those days. Clem Burke or people from Television or Heartbreakers. Everyone knew each other at one point, because everyone would run into each other. And that's how I got to know Dee Dee, because how many places do you go? You hang out in two different places, you're bound to get to know each other.

So, he told me that Tommy wanted to leave the band. So I said, "Does that mean you need another Tommy?" And he said, "Yeah, I'd like you to play with me, play with us."

So, from Richard Hell, which you heard of, to the Ramones. I joined the band at that point. And John came to Max's one night and told me that I was in the band, so it's legitimate.

*How did you adapt your own drumming style to the Ramones'?*

**MARKY:** Well, they gave me tapes of the demos [for *Road to Ruin*] and also *Alive!* sets that I had to know in two weeks, because they were already doing an American tour, and then from there a European tour. So, I had to learn *Road to Ruin* real quick on a pair of headphones and a drum pad, and I just played along with it. I just played what I'd play to it.

*Did you find it difficult to adjust to the Ramones' thing?*

**MARKY:** I was already doing, I guess, 5/4 and a lot of drum fills with Richard Hell and the Voidoids. But drumming to the Ramones was trying to drum the eighth notes on the double hi-hat, and that was pretty hard, because you're just constantly drumming like a machine. It took about a month or two to adjust to the band, and then after that it came pretty easily, surprisingly.

**JOEY:** But Marc, when he joined the band, the band became much heavier. I was always very impressed with Marc's drumming. He's one of my favorite drummers. To me, he's up there with Keith Moon or Ginger Baker.

**MARKY:** Wow. Keith Moon was real unique as a drummer. I guess he started all that double bass drum, Ginger Baker, Louie Bellson type of thing. But he really [had] showmanship, with real awe-inspiring stuff. I really liked Mitch Mitchell from Jimi Hendrix, guys like that, and John Bonham was really unique as a drummer. Those were the guys I liked. Comparing with them is pretty flattering coming from Joey.

*Yeah. Obviously, they appreciate your talents there. I think the first time I really noticed how unique your drum style is, was of all things, you did a walk-on on* The David Letterman Show *to do a Top Ten List. Your drumming there transformed the band into an entirely different sound. I thought that was an amazing accomplishment.*

**MARKY:** Yeah. They told me to come down for that, and I was just doing a military snare drum roll that I picked up in a military band in high school. That's really all it really was. And then we did "Take Me Out to the Ball Game" and it was Ramones style, basically with constant eighth notes. It was a lot of fun to do that.

*I'm surprised that Johnny never had the band cover "Take Me Out to the Ball Game."*

**MARKY:** Yeah, I know. He's really into collecting baseball memorabilia, and he knows all about that stuff.

*Marky's first record with the Ramones is* Road to Ruin. *By now, the songs are starting to get a little longer, and the band sounds a little* heavier. *The album itself sounds a little more downbeat than the first three. Was that conscious, or...?*

**JOHNNY:** You know more about this than me, I'll tell ya [laughs].

*[laughs] Well, I've been a fan, I've been on the outside. You're on the inside, so you know how it happened. I just study it.*

**JOHNNY:** You know, we try to step away and look at it, but when you're that close, sometimes it's hard to notice a change in the theme of the album. To me, we just write another twelve Ramones songs, whatever, and go in and record it. We didn't really notice any different feel, until I would read reviews saying that it was kind of downbeat.

**JOEY:** Well, the band became stronger. We worked on that with Tom and Ed again. By that point it was more of a coproduction thing. I guess me and Dee Dee were individually writing most of the songs, but there were band collaborations as well. I wrote "I Wanna Be Sedated" and Dee Dee [with "Don't Come Close" and "Questioningly"] was kind of experimenting more in, I don't know, I guess country music or something like that [laughs].

**JOHNNY:** We tried out two songs, which I don't like at all at this point, "Questioningly" and "Don't Come Close." The Ramones have always had a little bit of leeway to try out some different things. We're not as stuck as some people might think, 'cause we've had pop songs, we've had ballads, we've had punk songs, we've done the occasional hardcore punk song. But we've always had a little bit of variety. People sometimes think with the Ramones, everything sounds the same. Otherwise, I don't really notice anything particularly downbeat, but I guess you notice it. There was no really different feeling within the band, it just came out that way. We always sort of sang downbeat type of songs, just sung cheerfully.

What particular songs are you looking at that would be downbeat?

*"I Wanted Everything," or even "I Wanna Be Sedated," which is really a bubblegum tune.*

**JOHNNY:** Yeah.

*"I Don't Want You," "I'm Against It," all of that. Or "I Just Want to Have Something to Do," which is like the best track KISS never did.*

**JOHNNY:** [laughs] "I Wanted Everything" is on that album? That's a good one. I like that one.

**MARKY:** To me, that's like the almost perfect album. Not because I did it, because I always liked what they were doing before I was in the band. There was a little bit of lead guitar in there, and the quality of the production was real good compared to the previous albums that they did. There was a little more time taken to do it, and I was very happy with the outcome of it.

*I recall hearing that album in its entirety on a radio station when it came out. At that time, it was possible to hear the Ramones on the radio every once in a great while.*

**JOEY:** Yeah, we were getting played. Actually, Vin Scelsa, I think, was the first. In New York City, WNEW-FM, Vin Scelsa was playing us, and we would get played a lot on that station. He was the first DJ to play punk rock, Scelsa. And I remember he'd play us, and he'd play the Pistols, he'd play the Clash and Patti Smith and all that. And it was great. I always enjoyed listening to his show, just sit and listen to him and all sorts of music.

*The one cover on* Road to Ruin *was the Searchers' "Needles and Pins." That was kind of a change of pace right there from previous covers.*

**JOEY:** Yeah, well we always went for more obscure songs to cover. Like "Let's Dance," Chris Montez. Actually, even for myself, because Tommy and John, they were a little more into some of the fifties things, more than I was. So, for me it was like a learning experience with some of the stuff, too. But then the Searchers were a favorite band of ours. And we did "Needles and Pins," and it came out really good.

*They were actually your labelmates around that time.*

**JOEY:** Yeah, right! They were with Sire, too. Also, like going back as far as the label went, the Ramones were the first band to give Sire their focus. Because up until we first signed with them, they had—I guess Focus was the band that kind of put them on the map, like "Hocus Pocus." Christine McVie and Climax Blues Band and Beaver Brown and a lot of compilation type of things.

*So, you put them on the road to Madonna, basically [laughs].*

**JOEY:** Yeah, we did! I mean, we gave 'em their focus.

*Sire was a very interesting label at the time, with a lot of great bands. I mean, between you and the Flamin' Groovies, you had two of my favorite seventies bands on one label.*

**JOEY:** Well, Seymour [Stein], he knew what was great. He always has known what was great, and he took chances. He gave people a shot that might not have gotten a shot at all [otherwise]. I mean, after signing the Dead Boys, and signing Richard Hell, and Sham 69, he put their album out....

*The Saints, Radio Birdman....*

**JOEY:** Yeah, a lot of great stuff.

*Before* Road to Ruin *came out, Greg Shaw wrote in* Bomp! *magazine that you'd recorded an earlier version of "Needles and Pins" with Tommy on drums.*

**JOHNNY:** Boy, I don't even remember that. I don't remember recording it with Tommy. I know it was a leftover track from somewhere else, so maybe it was from the *Rocket to Russia* album, huh? It might have been a leftover track, and then we may have rerecorded it. We were happy, you know, we had done it well. Usually, I'm not happy with covers at all, but that one came out well.

*The next album was* It's Alive!, *a double live album recorded with Tommy, but not issued in the US*

**JOEY:** Yeah, we wanted to do a live album, and we were like really big in England at the time. And we played, it was New Year's Eve 1977, and it was a real big show at the Rainbow Theatre. And I guess everybody was there, all the bands at that point. Ya know, the whole audience was mostly bands [laughs], like the Clash, the Pistols, everybody was there.

And so we recorded that night. And Ed Stasium, I think he did the recording. It was a mobile situation. And it came out great! I remember, I think it was *NME* that said it was the best live album ever recorded. Previously it was Thin Lizzy. Yeah, it's never been released in America. [**NOTE:** It's Alive! *was finally released in the US in 1995. About friggin' time!*]

**JOHNNY:** Yeah, it's been released in some countries in its complete form on CD, in Europe, France. We're trying to get it released in America. Sire just keeps postponing it.

*Why in the world wasn't it released here at the time?*

**JOHNNY:** Knowing the truth is really hard. They'll say to you, "Well, it's not really time in America for a live album. We'll just wait until you guys are a little bigger." But I don't know if they had some sort of deals with the European people and all. I don't believe anything anyone tells me as far as the record company or the record industry.

*Let me get this straight: It's 1979, just a few years after Peter Frampton, KISS, and Bob Seger had their commercial breakthroughs via live sets, and the very same year that Cheap Trick became huge with their live album* Cheap Trick at Budokan. *So, these were all recent success stories of career-making live albums in America. And the record company says that the time's not right for a live album in America?!*

**JOHNNY:** That's what we were saying at the time. But they kept saying, "We want another studio album, we want another studio album." Meanwhile, it still goes unreleased. It will eventually be out, I'm sure, on CD. I don't understand why they won't put it out. They probably have some sort of deal going on with Europe, getting back some money from them, or something or another. A lot of fishy stuff goes on.

**JOEY:** Well, they're talking about putting it out this year. Coming in April they're gonna put out everything that hasn't previously been [reissued].

Actually, we shot some live [footage], the show was filmed, too, the New Year's Eve show. [It's] out on the fringe somewhere, somewhere out there. Maybe Danny Fields has it. *[NOTE: The* It's Alive! *video footage was eventually released as part of a 2007 DVD package called* It's Alive 1974–1996.*]*

*Also, in '79, the Ramones made their film debut in* Rock 'n' Roll High School. *How did you wind up as film stars?*

**JOHNNY:** I don't know, [director Allan] Arkush contacted us. From what I've heard, Cheap Trick rejected the movie. They asked if they could come down and see us play. We set up a job someplace uptown, [at] Hurrah's or something like that. We played the show, and they wanted us.

**JOEY:** We were out, we were touring, and Roger Corman asked us to be in this film, *Rock 'n' Roll High School.* And Allan Arkush was director, and he was a really big Ramones fan. He told me the day he kind of had the idea for this film, I guess he always daydreamed about doing a film with the Yardbirds, ya know?

So, when he got the opportunity to make the film, he changed it. Initially, Corman wanted it to be a disco movie, 'cause, ya know, his films are cars and girls and all that. So, [Arkush] substituted the disco and the blown-up cars and the whole bit for us [laughs].

But actually, it was an all-star Corman cast. It was a real classic film. It really created a whole new genre of film after that point, because then a lot of all these teen films started comin' out and stealing little bits and pieces of *Rock 'n' Roll High School*. But it was a great experience to do it. It felt really kind of strange because we had never done anything like this before. So, you almost felt like really kind of alien.

**MARKY:** It wasn't fun making the movie. You sit around all day waiting for them to call you, and then you could just be doing one little thing for a half hour, an hour, and that's it for the day. You sit around like ten or eleven hours.

**JOHNNY:** Well, looking back at it, it's great. At the time, not particularly much fun, because you had to be there early, you had to sit around all day waiting for your part. It was sort of torturous. The people were all real nice to us, though, everyone involved with the film. But the movie, you sit around all day and just wait for your part, and it's just boring and monotonous. And that was probably a fast-paced movie! I can imagine on big-budgeted things they must not do any work. Nothing goes fast enough for me, and that was really slow.

**JOEY:** It's become a real classic film. We got friendly with [actors] Mary Woronov and Paul Bartel. I mean, there were a lot of great people on the film. And [actress] P. J. Soles, of course. [After the film came out], everybody wanted to meet P. J. Soles.

**JOHNNY:** So, looking back at it, great. You know, I was in a film, and that film is actually…people feel like it's a good rock 'n' roll film. I saw it in a screening when they first completed the film. It was just us and a few people who were invited. And it's just, "Oh, shit, this movie's terrible. This could ruin our career." I don't find nothing funny at all, and I was, like, *depressed.*

And then they opened it up at the Eighth Street Playhouse there, and I waited for the movie to start. I went in, and I stood in the back of the theater. And the whole place was all full, and the kids were all laughing at everything. And I said, "Oh, great, they like it!"

*It's funny, actually. I remember the first time I saw it. It played here in Syracuse on July 6 of '79. They played it at a club, Uncle Sam's on Erie Boulevard East, and we all stood through the whole movie. Then a local band, the Flashcubes, played, and then you came on and played. Five bucks went a long way in '79.*

**JOHNNY:** I remember the Flashcubes, I remember them. So, did it go over okay?

*Oh, yeah, it was great. It was terrific, it got great local press.*

**JOHNNY:** You sit there watching it by yourself and you just think it's really corny, really terrible....

*Yeah, but that's the whole point.*

**JOHNNY:** I guess so [laughs]!

*Did you ever consider making another movie?*

**JOHNNY:** I don't rule nothing out, but I'm not looking forward to it. If there's the right offer. We're not actors, you know. It's hard for me to watch myself doing it, because I'm going, "Oh, God, it's awful!" We come off like aliens within the film, so I guess it's okay. We're so alien to everybody else in the film, so our bad acting is actually good.

**JOEY:** Well, we got a lot of offers for things that were similar, but you don't wanna do that. I mean, what we did was original and classic, ya know? And [Martin] Scorsese hasn't really offered us a part, ya know? [laughs] But actually, it's funny, because he did a film recently and we're on the soundtrack. It's called *Naked in New York*.

*What did you think of the* Rock 'n' Roll High School *soundtrack album?*

**MARKY:** Under the circumstances, I thought it came out okay. I think that the song selections for the movie was good. I liked the live tracks for the *Loco Live* better, and the Ramones' *It's Alive!* But I think that, for what it was, it came out pretty good.

**JOHNNY:** They asked us to record two new songs, one ballad and the theme song from the movie. We did "I Want You Around" and "Rock 'n' Roll High School." We had done a demo of "I Want You Around"—I don't know where it is—that was much, much better than what we ended up putting on the record.

**JOEY:** We had done a version of "I Want You Around" that John played—at that point, he had a '57 Rickenbacker, like the same one that John Lennon had—and it really came out amazing. It had, like, an early Rolling Stones feel. And that version was supposed to be on the [*All the Stuff (And More), Volume* Two] CD, but there was another version put on [instead]. Accidentally, actually.

**JOHNNY:** I don't know what the other one sounds like, the one that got issued on the recent CD. I don't think I've listened to it yet. I don't listen to the stuff much [laughs].

*You've done it and moved on.*

**JOHNNY:** I hear a song sometimes, I'm in a record store and they put the album on, and I go, "I don't remember doing that song!" I don't remember doing it.

*Well, were ya there that day in the studio, Johnny?*

**JOHNNY:** Yeah, I probably learned the song the day before I went in and just recorded it, and that was probably the last time I ever played it, you know?

We also recorded "C'mon Let's Go" [with the Paley Brothers]. Joey was, I don't know where he was. He was incapacitated.

**JOEY:** It was a single before it was on the soundtrack. I was laid up, and John and Tommy and Dee Dee, they did the track with the Paley Brothers singin' the lead. It sounded very Everly Brothersish. I thought it came out great. [*NOTE:"C'mon Let's Go" was recorded circa 1977, when Joey was sidelined by second- and third-degree burn injuries.*]

**JOHNNY:** Seymour said, "Will you go in and play a song and have the Paley Brothers sing it?" I think he wanted "C'mon Let's Go." And I said, "What, are you gonna pay us or something?" You know, we want some money. And he said, "Uhhhh…."

We negotiated a hundred bucks each [laughs], big money. And I said, "Great! Hundred bucks for the night here, I'll go in and do it." Went in, put the record on, had Tommy figure out how to play it, [and he] showed me how to play it. I think I did two takes and said, "That's it, that's as good as I'm gonna play it. I'm done." And it came out good. The faster you do it, the better it comes out.

*Before* Rock 'n' Roll High School, *Joey was in* Punk *magazine's photo-funnies special "Mutant Monster Beach Party." Joey wrote the lyrics for that, and a lot of those lyrics turned up later, divided between "Rock 'n' Roll High School" and "Danny Says."*

**JOEY:** Yeah, well, I remember *Punk* magazine was very supportive of the band. We were good friends with [*Punk* magazine masterminds] John Holmstrom and Legs [McNeil] at the time, and that "Mutant Monster Beach Party" was a lot of fun. It was kind of like a movie in a magazine, ya know? And one day I got inspired and started writing, like, a theme kind of a title track for *Mutant Monster Beach Party*. And so, I had this kind of a song partially written.

And when Allan Arkush said he wanted us to write the title track for *Rock 'n' Roll High School*, I told him that I had this thing that I had partially written. Actually, the music, I had finished the music and most of the words. And I just changed it from "Mutant Monster Beach Party"—I don't remember the words completely— and substituted 'em with "Rock 'n' Roll High School."

*Phil Spector remixed the studio tracks for the soundtrack album. Was that your first involvement with Spector?*

**JOEY:** Ed had done the demo sessions for us out in LA. In those days, every time we'd go out to Los Angeles, Phil would be at the shows, and he'd come backstage. And he'd always be buggin' us about how he wanted to produce an album for us. He would always say, "Do you want to make a great album, or just a good one?" implying that if we didn't work with him, our album would only be, ya know, decent.

**JOHNNY:** We wanted to get Phil at that point, keep him involved. Phil had wanted to do us, I think, almost back to *Rocket to Russia*. I remember definitely *Road to Ruin*. We kept trying to postpone it. We really did not want to work with Phil. He had done his thing in the sixties, in the early- to mid-sixties. We wanted to maintain as much control over it as possible. We had serious apprehensions about working with him.

**JOEY:** So, the way the Phil thing really came about was initially he wanted to do a solo album with me. And in those days, it was a little premature. And I really wanted to try working with Phil. We kind of gave it a shot. It was an experiment.

**JOHNNY:** By the time *Road to Ruin* came, we realized that, as far as becoming big, there was trouble. That punk was not taking off. Punk was already dead at that point as far as the whole movement.

And we felt that maybe we needed to work with him. Maybe we needed to work with a big name for the help his name would bring.

*What was it like to make* End of the Century *with Spector?*

**JOHNNY:** Torture, torture. He'd be nice to us, but he'd be so horrible to everyone around. And I don't care if he's being nice to me. I'm sure Joey is gonna feel different; he's like their idol, Joey and Marc. But if the person isn't a nice guy, I don't care if I liked his work. It doesn't mean anything. And if he's being nice to me but horrible to everybody else, still he's not a nice guy.

**MARKY:** Well, Phil was, I guess, an overanxious perfectionist, and he would just sit there and listen to one or two things all night long. I guess he was looking for some kind of drum sound or kind of tone on the guitar or whatever. He just seemed confused sometimes when he was fighting with Harry, the engineer—Larry [Levine], I'm sorry. It would always end up like that. We would go to the studio about seven, eight o'clock at night, and we'd end up leaving around six, seven in the morning the next day, the next morning. We were used to working fast, and he was into working kind of slow.

So, it took about six weeks to do this. And it really got to the point where we were all at our wits' end. I would end up going barhopping with Phil at night, drinking, drinking wine all night just to get out of the boredom. But then the next day, we would have to be in the studio, so I don't think that really helped the situation. His way of working was a little different than what we were used to, let's say, working with Ed Stasium or Tommy Ramone.

**JOEY:** A lot of people loved it and a lot of people felt it wasn't…right for the Ramones, let's say. I guess Seymour wanted to give it a shot, and also I guess there was maybe some kind of aspect of making the band a little more commercial or something. To me, it was kind of a historical coupling in a sense, it was [melodramatic voice] "the coming together of two walls." A real clash.

*The wall of sound meets the wall of noise.*

**JOEY:** [laughs]

**JOHNNY:** It was torturous. It was incredibly slow going, no communication with whatever was bothering him with the takes and all. He'd just stamp around the room and tell you to do it again, and listen to it for three hours, and then come back and do it again. He wouldn't even do multiple takes, just one every three hours. You couldn't get into any rhythm of the whole thing. I don't like the album. I don't like the production. The songs are probably fine; with Ed producing it, it probably would have been a fine album.

**JOEY:** For me, personally, I really enjoyed it. I learned a lot. I felt that I wrote some of my best songs on that album, "Danny Says" and "Do You Remember Rock 'n' Roll Radio?" and "I'm Affected." It was a very inspirational time for me. I was living at the Tropicana Hotel with a woman, and it was just a very high time for me.

I mean, I'm glad Phil Spector produced that record, because if he didn't, it would never have sounded the way it came out. "Danny Says" would never have sounded that way if somebody else would have done it. And Ed Stasium was there. I mean, it really had that intensity.

**MARKY:** To this day, I'm not really happy with the drum sounds on the album. Looking back, I guess at the time that's what Phil wanted.

*Why did you decide to record "Chinese Rock"?*

**JOHNNY:** It was our song. Dee Dee had brought it to us at the time of probably *Leave Home*. At that time, we were doing "53rd & 3rd" and "Commando." To me, there were similarities. He had just come up with a song that was similar to the other two in some ways.

It also was mentioning dope. And we didn't mind singing about certain drugs, but we didn't wanna sing about dope. Certain drugs, we thought—LSD, we didn't think anybody did LSD, we didn't think it was around anymore, so it's okay to sing about LSD. There's no problem. But we didn't wanna sing about dope, so we avoided it. The Heartbreakers then started doing it, and we realized it was a good song. I didn't like the way our version came out. [The Heartbreakers'] version was better.

**JOEY:** "Chinese Rock" didn't come out the way it should have. I don't think Phil would be the right choice for producer for a song like that. It lacked the aggression that it needed.

**JOHNNY:** And "Baby I Love You," I didn't play on that. Once they were bringing in an orchestra, I said, "I ain't sticking around." Yeah, Joey and the orchestra. That's the worst song we've ever done, I believe. That's a black mark that still bothers me.

*Yet it was the Ramones' biggest-ever hit in England.*

**JOHNNY:** That probably makes it even worse. It probably took care of our career in England at that point.

**JOEY:** "Baby I Love You" was, I think, Top 8 or something like that. Earlier on, "Blitzkrieg Bop," "I Wanna Be Your Boyfriend," "Sheena" was a Top 10 hit. The albums were all Top 20 albums. [**NOTE:** *According to the book* British Hit Singles, *"Baby I Love You" was the only Ramones single to crack the British Top 10, reaching # 8. "Sheena Is a Punk Rocker" was the Ramones' highest-charting British single otherwise, and it peaked at # 22.* End of the Century *was also the only Ramones album to reach the UK Top 20, peaking at #14.*]

*But you were prophets without honor in your homeland.*

**JOEY:** No. I mean, people were really excited by us overseas. We were like a breath of fresh air for them, and they were waiting for [it]. Like in England, every week pretty much there'd be something new happening, I guess, [but] later on. So, up until *Rocket to Russia,* we were darlings of the scene. But we earned it, ya know?

*Then the British press seemed to turn on you.*

**JOEY:** They turned on us on *Road to Ruin*. But then they apologized after the damage was done. "Oh, this album is great!," ya know? And in those days, the press was so powerful in England—it's still pretty powerful—but there was a point where the reviews really kind of decided if the album was going to sell or not, or flop. The English press have always been sort of famous for destroying careers, and making and breaking, let's say.

*"Do You Remember Rock 'n' Roll Radio?" was the first of the radio critiques from the Ramones.*

**JOEY:** Yeah. It was about disenchantment with the state of radio. Ya know, growin' up on radio and it being really important, it turned you on to all the great artists. And then radio, it became big business. It seemed like it was just happening in America, but it was really happening all over the world.

*Some of the lyrical themes on the album seem more overtly political than the Ramones had ever been before. "All the Way" and "High Risk Insurance" in particular show more of a right-wing political bent.*

**JOEY:** Right. Well, those songs were written by [John]. John was a Republican. Dee Dee would flip-flop. Me and Marc, in those days...the breakdown, John's a Republican, I'm a Democrat, Marc's a Democrat.

There was a real growth of self, I would say, you know what I mean? That's the best way to describe it for me anyway. But yeah, I mean earlier on with the logo...we were, you know, patriots....

*It probably reflected the mood of the country at the time.*

**JOEY:** Right. Well, Dee Dee, that was kind of where his head was at in those days.

And moving along....

*Do you think that Sire expected* End of the Century *to sell better than it did? Do you think that Sire got what they expected out of it?*

**JOEY:** Well, I was disappointed because I thought…I mean, actually it wasn't the first album that disappointed me [laughs]. I felt very frustrated by putting out great albums and seeing them not really happen.

Ya know, actually I remember with *End of the Century* being kind of pissed off because, ya know, like Seymour, the fact that we got to work with Phil…and then I remember the Pretenders being signed, and their album getting the push and *End of the Century* kind of not getting any push. And just thinking, ya know, it was kind of a perfect album to succeed. Whereas in Holland, I think "Rock 'n' Roll High School" was a Top 5 single, and I guess in Australia "Rock 'n' Roll High School" was like a Top 5 hit single, and in Japan, as well.

So, I mean, even at the time things were kinda fucked up, as far as at times you didn't really know what was going on completely. And whether the label was really doing what they should've been doing for you.

Pleasant Dreams, *produced by 10cc's Graham Gouldman, is a true anomaly among Ramones albums. It doesn't sound like any other Ramones album.*

**JOHNNY:** Yeah, this is the low point of our career here. We were just told that management is trying to find us a producer. He found out nobody was interested. I don't know if that's true or not. It's Gary [Kurfirst], which is still our manager.

**JOEY:** I remember when we were in England, and I heard *So Alone*, the Johnny Thunders solo record. Steve Lillywhite produced it. I think it might have been one of the earliest things that he had produced. And I remember thinking, "This is great, I'd really like to work with him."

And mentioning it to management! At this point, we'd just changed management. We'd let Danny go, and we took on Gary Kurfirst. And I mentioned Steve Lillywhite, and the response was, "What kind of track record does he have?" Which I couldn't understand because I thought the idea of making records was working with exciting new people, fresh new people, fresh new ideas.

So, Sire really wanted us to be working with somebody who maybe could break the band. So, they went kind of to the other extreme for this very commercial kind of guy.

**JOHNNY:** Basically, [Graham Gouldman] was the only person they could get. And I knew it was going to be bad because the guy from 10cc producing the Ramones? 10cc sucks, and it's not right for the Ramones. As soon as I started playing, he goes, "You're getting too much distortion in your guitar, you gotta turn down your volume." I go, "I've done five or six albums like this, this is nothing!" I could see we weren't on the same wavelength at all.

**JOEY:** But I think part of the reason they chose Graham Gouldman was because of his success with the Yardbirds. He wrote so many great songs for the Yardbirds and the Hollies and people of that nature. And I know we also had discussed producing that album by ourselves, which they weren't for that idea either. They told us, "Your album's gonna flop unless we work with Graham." It kinda flopped anyway [laughs].

**MARKY:** I happen to like that album a lot. A lot of people don't like it because it's our pop album. John doesn't like it. Me and Joey like it. I don't know whether Dee Dee liked it or not. I'm not sure. But I really liked it a lot.

The situation was real good. It was [recorded] in New York, Immediate Studios, a big room. I liked working with Graham Gouldman. He was involved with the Yardbirds, he wrote some stuff with them. It was done in the spring of 1980, and it came out in '81.

I happened to like that a lot. We worked quick and it was a lot of fun to do.

**JOEY:** He made us very pop. I mean, some of the songs came out great. But it didn't have the edge. I remember doing the demos with Ed Stasium, and them sounding so fuckin' amazing. Like, "The KKK Took My Baby Away" we did with Ed, and it had so much aggression and it was great. It didn't come off that way on the album.

**JOHNNY:** Nobody in the band was talking to each other at that point. I didn't get to cowrite any songs with Dee Dee, so we were short on punk songs. 'Cause Dee Dee always wrote great lyrics, but he had some problems with the music end. So, a lot of the real punk songs [on previous albums], like "Cretin," "Lobotomy," that kind of stuff, were all things that me and Dee Dee had written. So [*Pleasant Dreams*] is sort of very lightweight with the production and the lacking of any punk songs.

*This was the first Ramones album with individual songwriting credits.*

**JOHNNY:** Right. This was leading to the whole breakdown here of the band at this point. All of a sudden, the egos were getting out of hand.

**JOEY:** Well, it was time to give credit where credit was due. I mean, four people don't write [together]. It kind of didn't make any sense. In the early days, okay—you're creating something, introducing something to the public. But when you write a song, you're putting yourself into it.

Four people don't write every song. It's kind of ridiculous. And when you're putting your own feelings or whatever it be, you want people to know.

*For the next album,* Subterranean Jungle, *you hooked up with producers Ritchie Cordell and Glen Kolotkin, known for their bubblegum work in the sixties.*

**JOEY:** Right. In this interim period here, we really didn't have a lot of say about who we would be working with. Like, Sire was pushing for us to have commercial success, and we really didn't have much to say about who we'd be working with. But we wanted somebody where we could get the edge back.

So, Kenny Laguna was mentioned, and he was working with Joan Jett at the time. He was producing and managing her. So, we started working with Kenny, but Kenny was too busy with Joan to comply. So, we worked with his partner, Ritchie Cordell, and Glen Kolotkin. And Ritchie was kind of famous for those bubblegum singles [laughs].

**JOHNNY:** Ritchie Cordell came down at one point. He was interested in producing it, and we could see that that wasn't going to work. At times, different people have gotten sort of desperate for hits. And I don't know, I didn't really care. I was more concerned with keeping the Ramones fans happy, and I don't want anything that's going to embarrass the Ramones' image. So, a lot of times it's been a struggle with trying not to go overboard and try to be commercial. Of course, you get pressure from record companies, you get pressure from management, so people start bending at times. And we can't worry about that.

**MARKY:** I didn't like *Subterranean Jungle*, but a lot of our fans liked that a lot compared to *Pleasant Dreams*. So, it depends on what you like, if you like real heavy punk or you like pop punk. I didn't like the production, and at that point I was not really happy with the way things were going.

**JOEY:** Personally, I thought it was one of the least strong albums. But over the years, a lot of people think it's one of their favorites. I think there's a lot of great songs on it: "Psycho Therapy," "Everytime I Eat Vegetables It Makes Me Think of You," "Outsider."

*It was the first Ramones LP to be deleted from the catalog.*

**JOHNNY:** It got deleted very quickly. I've always considered that odd because it wasn't selling a whole lot, but it wasn't that much different in sales. I mean, you still have your Ramones base, and they go out and buy the album. So, all of a sudden that got deleted.

There's songs on it I like a lot. There's some stuff I don't like. We did two covers on that. Three covers, actually, with the Boyfriends' song "I Need Your Love." I heard the Boyfriends do the song. They did it great, and then we tried it and didn't do it very well. [The Music Machine's] "Little Bit O' Soul," that didn't come out very good. I don't like [the Chambers Brothers'] "Time Has Come Today," [but] that felt passable, I guess. We also did [the 1910 Fruitgum Company's] "Indian Giver" on that album, but they didn't include it. We probably would have been better off with that, because that one came out good. We probably would have been better off to leave off "I Need Your Love" and put "Indian Giver" on, or something like that.

"Psycho Therapy" is on [*Subterranean Jungle*], which is a good song. Something else that's on there that's really good I like....

*"Outsider"?*

**JOHNNY:** I like that, but it's not the one I was thinking of. Do you have the album there?

*Yeah. "In the Park" was my favorite at the time.*

**JOHNNY:** That's not it either.

*"Timebomb"? "What D'ya Do"? "Highest Trails Above"?*

**JOHNNY:** "Highest Trails," yeah, that one I like. Crazy song.

**JOEY:** We did ["Indian Giver"], but I've forgotten what exactly was the reason behind that they didn't want it to be released. I really don't remember actually. But we wound up putting it out later on *Ramones Mania*. Actually, it came out real good.

*Joan Jett also covered that, but it seems the Ramones' version is definitive.*

**JOEY:** Well, I think with us, the Ramones, we're an original band. What we do comes naturally to us. It's not like, "Let's do a bubblegum song, let's do this," you know what I mean? With a lot of other artists, ya know, you listen when they do a cover song, and it's like they're trying to do this cover song. It doesn't flow naturally. You notice when it comes from the real place.

I mean, bubblegum was an inspiration of ours, definitely an influence. It was funny to find out later on that Glen Kolotkin had produced the Chambers Brothers, had conceived that sound, that kind of almost Sensurround type of production on "Time Has Come Today."

*"Time Has Come Today" is like a textbook example of a band and a cover that you'd never think could possibly work together, yet it does. It's like a dry run for 1994's* Acid Eaters *album.*

**JOEY:** It worked. Well, it's a great song.

*There was a report in* CREEM *magazine that you'd recorded a track with Petula Clark for the album. Was there ever any truth to that?*

**JOEY:** Actually, it was Lesley Gore. Well, we didn't wanna do this. It was…whose idea was it? I think it was Ritchie's. We were working at Kingdom, it was a studio out in Long Island. And Lesley Gore worked there, too, she did her business from there. And she cowrote this song that I think they tried passing off on Joan Jett, but she for whatever reason wasn't interested. So, I think we tried it, but it wasn't right for us either.

Actually, Girlschool wound up doing it. I don't remember the name of the song. I don't think it was on an album, it was on a single. [**NOTE:** *It was "1-2-3-4 Rock and Roll," written by Jeanne Napoli, Lesley Gore, Benjy King, and Rick Blakemore, produced by Cordell and*

Kolotkin, released in 1983 as the title track for a Girlschool EP.] I mean, it's a good song, it was a good song for them. It's just, I remember the vocals were like super-high vocals. It was kind of ridiculous.

**JOHNNY:** [*Subterranean Jungle*] was a step back, a step in the right direction following *Pleasant Dreams*.

**JOEY:** I guess by that period in the band there was a lot of infighting. It was kind of like it wasn't a great period. I mean, it's never been easy in the band, there's always been a lot of shit [laughs]. But at that period especially, there was a lot going on. We were having some problems with Marc at that point. It was a weird [time], very strange.

**MARKY:** I was really into drinking a lot. They were not happy with my situation, so it was better that I left the band at that point. There was fighting in the band. Johnny and Dee Dee weren't getting along very well. There were all these arguments, and Joey and John weren't getting along too well. It was a depressing time for me, and I think getting out of the band for the three or four years that I was out of the band was sort of like a relief.

**JOHNNY:** Marc was an alcoholic, and his drinking got too bad. It was impossible during the *Subterranean Jungle* album. We had to actually bring in another drummer to play on "Time Has Come Today." He wasn't playing well, and it was bad. He had reached a bad point in his life. And he recovered, which is good. But we had to get rid of him.

Richie was the first person to come down and try out. He was fine, and we went with Richie.

*Before the next album, the Ramones contributed a track called "Chop Suey" to the soundtrack of a movie called* Get Crazy. *The track was produced by Busta Jones.*

**JOHNNY:** Oh, horrible track. I don't even know if I'm on it anymore. I don't hear me on it. I played, but I don't hear it. I don't know whose harebrained idea that was—probably Gary's [laughs]. Bad idea.

**JOEY:** Allan [Arkush]'s next film was *Get Crazy*. I had written a song called "Chop Suey." Originally, I had got the B-52s to sing on it, and there was some kind of a problem. And then Flo and Eddie sang on it [instead]. So, eventually maybe we can put out that [original] record.

*There was a report around that time that you were going to be doing an album with Busta Jones.*

**JOEY:** I don't think it was really true. Around that period, I was hangin' out with Busta Jones and Jerry Harrison. I was hanging out at Electric Lady with them, and the B-52s, and he was working with them. He mentioned about, you know, doing a song with us, and that's really how ["Chop Suey"] came about. And initially the B-52s were singing background on those parts, the "Chop Suey" parts.

**JOHNNY:** The song sucked, right [laughs]?

*Many have referred to your next album* Too Tough to Die *as your return to form.*

**JOHNNY:** That was probably the Ramones' best album of the eighties. The band started to communicate a little bit better, we were getting along a little bit better at that point.

**JOEY:** And also, at that point we told Sire—you know, we were renegotiating our contract—and we told them we were going to do things our way from there on in. So, we did *Too Tough to Die*. And the album was pretty dark and apocalyptic, but it reflected the times: the Iranian situation and Khomeini, the whole nuclear thing. It was pretty scary times. And the album, I think it's a great record and all, and it heavily reflected what was happening at that period, 1984. It was like another world [laughs].

**JOHNNY:** Yeah, I'm happy with the album. The production's good, the songs are good. It's a good album. It's one of our better albums.

*One track was produced by Busta Jones.*

**JOEY:** Right, "Chasing the Night." I had written that with Dee Dee and Jerry Harrison, and Busta was involved. And actually it was a little bit more experimental, a little heavier maybe. It was fun, it was fun doing that.

*And Dee Dee brings the Ramones to their first flirtation with hardcore, reaping the benefits of what you helped to create.*

**JOEY:** Yeah, Dee Dee was into hardcore at that point with "Wart Hog" and "Danger Zone." It was cool.

**JOHNNY:** Yeah, I think "Endless Vacation," especially. "Wart Hog" is…I don't know if it's hardcore, it's close. I guess maybe it's close. But "Endless Vacation" is. We started seeing the hardcore bands doing what they're doing, and people started saying, "Oh, the hardcore bands play faster than the Ramones," or whatever. "You guys don't play as fast." And we just wanted to show them that we could do hardcore better than anybody if that's what we're choosing to do.

The whole thing is in songs, and hardcore bands mostly are short on songs. So, we just wrote "Endless Vacation" to show them we can do it, too.

"Wart Hog" I like a lot, that's a good one. Me and Dee Dee had written that. I had the chorus of "Wart Hog," Dee Dee just had total different lyrics on a sheet of paper. They fit. I said, "Here's where the singing goes," he just sang his lyrics off the sheet of paper. The song was all done in a few minutes.

**JOEY:** On *Too Tough to Die*, we also worked with Dave Stewart on "Howling at the Moon," which was fun. I always enjoyed working with different people. I mean, I enjoyed working with Tom and Ed together. They produced a great record and it was exciting. But it was always kind of fun to work with various people.

On *Too Tough to Die*, as well as on *Subterranean Jungle*, we had Walter Lure [of the Heartbreakers]. He'd give us a helping hand on some additional guitar work. I guess on *Too Tough to Die*, I remember writing that song "No Go," trying my hand at a kind of a rockabilly style. Based on a true experience: sometimes when your brain wants to go, your feet won't.

*That's every waking moment of my life.*

**JOEY:** [laughs] Or your feet wanna go, but your brain don't [laughs].

*After* Too Tough to Die, *a couple of British singles appeared with tracks that hadn't yet been on any album. The first of these was the "Chasing the Night" single, which had a B-side featuring "Smash You," written by Richie, and a cover of the Rolling Stones' "Street Fighting Man."*

**JOHNNY:** "Smash You," I don't remember. I don't even remember the song.

"Street Fighting Man" was, to me, a disaster. We put down the basic track of that. I had wanted Dee Dee to sing the song. All of a sudden, somebody came in and put a guitar overdub there, Joey's singing, the song was all done without me, and they didn't even let me know they were doing it. And the only way I wanted to do the song to begin with was I envisioned Dee Dee singing a punk version of it. And it didn't turn out at all like I was expecting. It would have been interesting hearing it, though, with Dee Dee.

**JOEY:** We'd been talkin' about tryin' it. We tried it, and we weren't really crazy about the outcome. We didn't think we really captured it. So, that's why we kind of avoided releasing it at any other point in time.

*There was a somewhat higher profile on the next single, "Bonzo Goes to Bitburg." Up to this point, that was the most overtly political track the Ramones had ever done.*

**JOEY:** Yeah, I guess with the Ramones, when we felt strongly enough, we responded. That's when it's honest. We're not a band to jump on trends and, "Oh, it's hip to be political," like the Clash, whatever.

'Cause I guess by that point, just about everybody'd be jumping on the political bandwagon. 'Cause that's what the [rock journalists] wanted. They ate that stuff up.

**JOHNNY:** I think Dee Dee was just trying to jump on the bandwagon of, especially in Europe, people were singing political type songs, and the whole political issue. Because basically, any songs we had prior to that [with] even any mention of politics were usually sort of conservative, right? We would sing songs about Vietnam and things like that, and they were always sort of pro those movements.

And all of a sudden this comes out, and it's sort of a left-type song. I think that was it, you know. Dee Dee, he was never liberal politically. But that song, I think he just decided to write about to see if it would get played.

**JOEY:** But it was a really fucked-up move, when Reagan went to the SS graves over there. I feel like he just slapped America in the face. So, Dee Dee wrote the song, but we pulled it all together, me and Jean [Beauvoir, former Plasmatics guitarist]. Well, Jean, I think he wrote the music, Dee Dee wrote the words, and we just, like, pulled it all together. And the song was written that night, after seeing it on the news, and released right away. I guess it came out first in England.

**JOHNNY:** I did not want to be doing any political songs. I didn't want to be bad-mouthing the president. I was upset by the cover; the English record company did that. I think they were trying to jump on anything to knock America in any way. I didn't wanna see Europeans doing it. It's okay for Americans to criticize ourselves, but I don't want the Europeans doing it. These people have enough problems of their own.

*What are your memories of the* Animal Boy *album? Are you happy with how it turned out?*

**JOEY:** It was a fun album to make. Jean Beauvoir produced it, who we knew from the Plasmatics.

**JOHNNY:** I like the songs, I don't like the production. The production's a little thin. I have to adjust the stereo to make it sound right to me. I like the songs, though. A lot of good songs on it: "Animal Boy," "Freak of Nature" is on there. What did you think of the album?

*I like it. To be frank with you, my favorite track was actually "Something to Believe In"....*

**JOHNNY:** Oh, God!

*Sorry. Should have been a hit single for you. Great video to go with it, too.*

**JOHNNY:** I can't make any comments because I don't like the song, so I don't know. "Something to Believe In"? Okay, I remember the song now. It was a single [laughs], it was a video.

*"Something to Believe In" seemed like it was poised to be a radio hit. Billboard gave it and its video a real nice write-up.*

**JOEY:** Yeah! I think it came out real good. It was fun.

**JOHNNY:** But overall [other than that song], I like the album, I just don't like the production.

**JOEY:** "Something in My Drink" I thought came out great. It was written by Richie and Dee Dee. Richie was a real talented guy. I thought he was a good drummer, but he was a really good songwriter, too. He was talented. I don't think all his songs were that great. I thought "Somebody Put Something in My Drink" was classic, and "I'm Not Jesus" was wild.

The way I approached "Something in My Drink," I wanted to kind of conjure up the feeling. Because Richie...we were in San Francisco, Berkeley I think, doing a show, and somebody put a tab of acid in Richie's beer. And he flipped out, they had to take him away. And he was never the same since. And I think also, back in those days, somebody was giving out joints, but there was like angel dust in 'em. Dee Dee even started flippin' out.

JOHNNY: "Apeman Hop" is on that, that was funny doing that with Jean Beauvoir. We'd say, "Well, we need some African dialogue here, Jean [laughs], can you go out there and quote some African?"

*"Hey, man, I'm from Queens!"*

JOHNNY: [laughs] And he's…no way is he having any part of that. So, we sent Dee Dee out there, or somebody, I forget, there was somebody else, and start making up dialogue for that. Sound effects.

*Speaking in tongues. No wait, that's Talking Heads. Next, you did one more album with Richie,* Halfway to Sanity.

JOHNNY: Is that the Bill Laszlo one?

*No, that was, let's see, produced by the Ramones with Daniel Rey.*

JOHNNY: Oh, okay.

*With "I Wanna Live," "Garden of Serenity," duet with Debbie Harry on "Go Lil' Camaro Go."*

JOHNNY: Uh-huh. What did you think?

*I didn't like it much at the time. "I Wanna Live," I think, is classic; it's classic late-eighties Ramones. The rest of it seems…it's actually not something I've listened to in quite some time. I actually don't remember a lot of the individual songs.*

JOEY: Yeah, [*Halfway to Sanity*] came out great. Daniel Rey came in as producer, and I think it was his first production attempt. And we had Joe Blaney [mix it]. I liked working with Joe, and me and Richie were involved with the production, as well. I think back in those days, we were working at Intergalactic, and Jorge [Esteban, engineer on *Halfway to Sanity*] worked there, too. *Halfway to Sanity* was a lot of fun to make, and I think it's a great record.

**JOHNNY:** I don't think I mind it. I think it was okay. You reach a point where it's hard to come up with an album as good as...you know, twelve or fourteen albums in, it's hard to come up with an album as good as *Rocket to Russia*. It's almost impossible.

*If it makes you feel any better, no one else has come up with an album as good as* Rocket to Russia *either.*

**JOHNNY:** [laughs] Yeah, you reach a point you just hope you have a good album and there's no real shit songs on it.

*Well, any record that can contain a track like "I Wanna Live" is certainly not gonna be on anybody's bottom list. That track itself was already a departure for the Ramones. The guitar sound on that was a lot different than maybe what people would have expected.*

**JOEY:** "I Wanna Live" is a great track. I liked "Garden of Serenity"; it's one of my favorite tracks. It had that kind of guitar, that kind of acid-type sound. And "Death of Me," all those were kind of those cocaine days, ya know? For me, anyway [laughs]. It's sort of my subconscious wrote that song in about five minutes.

**JOHNNY:** Basically, I thought the album was okay. There were a lot of complaints while we were doing it within the band and with the production. I think Joey was complaining that Daniel was mixing the guitar too loud and he said the vocals weren't loud enough. What was Joey's comments on the album?

*He liked it. He especially liked "Garden of Serenity."*

**JOHNNY:** "Garden of Serenity" is good. I don't remember what else is on the album. Do you have the album there?

*Yes. Let's see..."Weasel Face," "Bop Till You Drop"....*

**JOHNNY:** "Weasel Face," I like "Weasel Face." "Bop Till You Drop," I like "Bop Till You Drop."

*Those are both classic, harder-edged Ramones stuff.*

**JOHNNY:** Richie had written a song or two on that. Is that with "Somebody Put Something in My Drink," or is that the album before that?

*That was on* Animal Boy.

**JOHNNY:** Yeah, there was something on that, too. "I'm Not Jesus" or something?

*"I'm Not Jesus" was on there.*

**JOHNNY:** What else?

*"Bye Bye Baby," "Worm Man," "I Lost My Mind," "Death of Me"….*

**JOHNNY:** "I Lost My Mind" I like. There was some stuff on there I like, some stuff on it I don't like. I reached a point where I'm kinda getting sick of the ballads. I probably wasn't liking "Bye Bye Baby." But it probably wasn't a bad ballad, but I'm getting a little tired of them already. "I'm Not Jesus" had that religious stuff that was going on. I like the song, I did not like the production on the song with the extra effects. I think any time you put extra stuff on, you get tired of it very quickly. I'm never for putting odd little things on, little gimmick things that you just get sick of.

*Of all the Ramones albums, I think it probably seems more like an eighties psychedelic record, more so than anything else the Ramones ever did. It's most noticeable on "Garden of Serenity," but it sounds like an MTV late-night* 120 Minutes/Alternative Nation *type of album, for good or ill. It sounds more of a piece with that than any other album the Ramones ever did.*

**JOHNNY:** Richie had written another song on that besides "I'm Not Jesus." What was the other song? There was one that I liked.

*Let's see here..."I Know Better Now."*

**JOHNNY:** Yeah. I think I liked that one. At least parts in it. It was interesting to play.

*What were the circumstances of Richie's departure from the band?*

**JOHNNY:** Richie leaving and Marky returning? Yeah, I remember that. What happened? Richie wanted to renegotiate his contract. Whatever he asked for was too high, we couldn't pay him what he was asking at that point. I just thought we'd reach some sort of compromise and just resolve the issue.

**JOEY:** Richie left suddenly. It was just some shit, ya know?

**JOHNNY:** Yeah, but somewhere Joey was out and supposedly said that we're throwing Richie out of the band. I think he says he didn't say it. It's really so difficult to get to the truth of this. But Richie had heard that Joey said we were throwing him out of the band, which was never discussed, we weren't doing that at all. We're not gonna start all over, it wasn't worth looking for a new drummer. So, all of a sudden, we play a show one night in Long Island, and his wife shows up with a limousine, picks him up, and says he's quitting. Gets in this limousine and drives off. Just like that. He heard we're throwing him out, he decided he's quitting before we throw him out. But that wasn't what was happening.

**JOEY:** Richie tried to screw us over. Because at the time of his leaving, we had a lot of important shows, and I guess he was out to sabotage us.

And Clem Burke stepped in. He joined the next day. And we knew Clem from Blondie, and we liked him, we liked his drumming.

**JOHNNY:** There was a lot of turmoil over this. Dee Dee says, "I'm quitting if Richie's not back with the band." Then, all of a sudden, he's up at the office and he hears that Clem Burke is interested in filling in or joining the band, and Dee Dee goes, "I want Clem Burke in the band." He forgot about Richie at that point [laughs]. Now he wants Clem Burke in the band. We rehearsed with Clem for about a week, played two shows. The shows did not go well at all—bad feeling. Clem is a real nice guy, and he's a good drummer, but he was not fitting in.

**JOEY:** It just didn't work out. He couldn't really handle our style. He was a different kind of drummer. He did two shows with us, two embarrassing shows [laughs]. I don't know, it was kind of exciting havin' him, but it just didn't work out.

**JOHNNY:** Maybe he needed more time to work, or more time to rehearse or whatever, I don't know. It may never have worked out, I don't know. I think we were desperate at this point here, and I felt we better come up with something quick here. And I heard that Marc had put a call in to someone, I think our road manager, and said that Marc was straight now for the past year or two, hadn't had a drink. And I thought, well, that's nice, it'd be nice to give the guy another chance. Fans would like to see back an old Ramone.

**MARKY:** I heard that Richie couldn't cut it anymore, so he decided to screw them by walking out on them. I thought he did some good stuff on some of the albums.

That's what happened at that point. I cleaned up, and I took about three, four years outside the business. I didn't want to be active. I wanted to stop the drinking problem that I had, because I couldn't stop if I was constantly touring. I had to have a support base in order to stop doing all that stuff.

Right before I joined the Ramones again, I had a band called King Flux with Richie Stotts of the Plasmatics. Then Monte [Melnick, the Ramones' long-suffering tour manager] called me and I got in the band again.

**JOHNNY:** This was a perfect situation. I told Marc [to] come down, and me and him rehearsed two, three songs, just me and him, and I said, "Marc, it's fine. Just like it was. You're in the band." Dee Dee goes again, "If you get rid of Clem, I'm quitting" again, and we go, "Well fine, Dee Dee, there's no choice. We got Marc so you decide what you want to do." [laughs] And that just blew over immediately.

**JOEY:** The idea of having Marc back in the band, ya know, Marc is pretty much an original member. At least I see him that way. And also, for the sake of the fans. People liked Marc. I always thought Marc was great, but it was even better [now]. He was very inspirational. It was great havin' him back.

*Next up was the compilation album,* Ramones Mania. *Does that stand up as the best of the Ramones?*

**JOHNNY:** I think so. There were some things on it that I didn't want on it, but....

*Like what?*

**JOHNNY:** Oh, I won't go through it. You know, the record company... we were reluctant to do it at a certain point because we wanted to make sure we were gonna pick the songs. We didn't want the record company picking the songs. We give them our list; they gave us their list. They gave us a list that's like nothing that's on the album, totally, twenty-five songs and we didn't even pick any of them. And we go, "What do you want us to do with this list? We didn't vote for any of these songs at all. We're not gonna get swayed on this, we want the songs that we want on." And we ended up agreeing on about four songs that they wanted on it. I'd have to look at the album to remember which ones.

*I could do it song by song, if you want.*

**JOHNNY:** You could mention some songs.

*"I Wanna Be Sedated."*

**JOHNNY:** Of course, we voted for that.

*"Teenage Lobotomy."*

**JOHNNY:** Yeah, we were for that.

*"Rock 'n' Roll Radio."*

**JOHNNY:** We voted for that.

*"Gimme Gimme Shock Treatment."*

**JOHNNY:** We voted for that.

*"Beat on the Brat."*

**JOHNNY:** We voted for that.

*"Sheena."*

**JOHNNY:** Yeah.

*"I Wanna Live."*

**JOHNNY:** Yeah, I'm sure we voted for that.

*"Pinhead."*

**JOHNNY:** Yeah.

*"Blitzkrieg Bop," obviously.*

**JOHNNY:** Yeah.

*"Cretin Hop."*

**JOHNNY:** Yeah.

*"Rockaway Beach."*

**JOHNNY:** Yeah.

*"Commando."*

**JOHNNY:** We might not have voted for that.

*Okay. "I Wanna Be Your Boyfriend."*

**JOHNNY:** We probably voted...we might not have voted for that [laughs]. So, do you feel it was a fair representation of the band?

*Do I think it is? Oh, yeah. Certainly, I don't think there's anybody who wouldn't have rearranged some tracks...*

**JOHNNY:** Oh, yeah.

*...any fan of any band.*

**JOEY:** We had a meeting with [Sire executive] Howie Klein. He had mentioned about putting it together, creating this album *Ramones Mania*. The idea was to kind of make it like a real collector's kind of album and choose different versions of the songs that hadn't been released. You know, not just put on what we felt were the best songs, but also to put on different versions that maybe people hadn't heard. Like, say "Rock 'n' Roll High School," there's about four different versions of "Rock 'n' Roll High School." There's the Phil Spector album, there's the soundtrack album, there's the film itself, and there were different mixes and things.

So, you wanted to kind of do something special for the collectors and the real fanatics and, you know, everybody. Just kind of create something cool. I mean, the song selection is great. And, also, on that album we put "Indian Giver."

**JOHNNY:** Right. They wanted a new song to put on the thing. What kind of gimmick is this, you know? I was totally against that. You want people to buy it because of one new song?

*Hey, it worked—I bought it! [laughs]*

**JOHNNY:** So that ["Indian Giver"] was already recorded. I wasn't about to record a brand-new one.

**MARKY:** I think it was pretty cool. That was pretty cool stuff in there, all the songs that, I guess, really represent the band compared to some of the other songs. But you could have made a Part Two a year later, with other songs, and it would have been just as good. We have so many songs and a lot of albums out that we could have a lot of choice because of how many songs we did. I thought that was pretty cool, that album.

**JOHNNY:** I remember reading some review, I don't remember who it was, I wonder if it was [*Village Voice* music critic Robert] Christgau or somebody like that. And he said, "I can't believe that they included 'Wart Hog' on this." I mean, we play "Wart Hog," "Wart Hog" is our most popular song that we play in the set. I was looking at it from fans' [viewpoint], and I'd ask kids, and these [critics] don't know. "Wart Hog" gets the best reaction when we play the show.

*"I Wanna Be Sedated" was pulled as a single from* Ramones Mania, *coupled on the 12" with its "Ramones on 45 Mega-Mix."*

**JOEY:** [laughs] Yeah, it was pretty amusing. I guess that was back in the days of "Stars on 45" and all that stuff. I remember hearing it at the old Ritz on Eleventh Street. It sounded really pretty wild. I think some DJ put that together, and that's how that came together. It wasn't like somebody's idea [in the band]. Back in those days, that was the day of the DJ and different mixing and dance mixes.

*The next proper album is* Brain Drain, *produced by Bill Laswell.*

**JOHNNY:** I guess I don't like the production. The album is okay, so-so. Not really—there aren't many really great songs, I don't think. "Pet Sematary," "Miracles." "Miracles" is very good.

*Terrific. Terrific single track.*

**JOHNNY:** Yeah, that's a great song. That one should have been a hit, I guess.

**JOEY:** Right. Well, that was a song that Dee Dee wrote, and yeah, that was a great song, too. It was kind of a universal feeling, ya know, a song of hope.

**MARKY:** I'd give [*Brain Drain*] about an eight, seven—seven and a half. I thought it came out good. I liked it better than *Subterranean Jungle*. I'm sure that's debatable for a lot of people. It had "Pet Sematary" on there, which is really good. In fact, a really perfect pop song. "The Girl Has Changed" was great on it. "Miracles" is real cool, and "UFO" is a real cool song.

**JOHNNY:** I don't feel like the album is bad. I'd give it a B [laughs], I'd give it a B. The production…he put, like, he had to put six to eight tracks of guitars on, and I don't see that way of doing it. I mean, I'm not gonna complain. If I'm not happy with the results, then I just won't work with him. I'm not gonna complain, give the guy a hard time. You hire him, let him do what he wants to do. I'm not for playing six to eight tracks of guitars. It's a lot of work, and it also just gets so layered I really can't distinguish what I'm playing. He was an alright guy, I liked him.

Joey didn't like him, did he? I don't think he would listen to his suggestions or something, I don't know.

**JOEY:** I wouldn't say it was one of the best albums, but it came out pretty good. And, also, we hooked up with Bill Laswell for that one. He didn't really want a whole lot of money to do it. He was a fan and he wanted to work with us. And we asked him, and he obliged us.

We liked the fact that he had worked with Motörhead and Iggy and Johnny Lydon's band, Public Image.

So, it came together. Actually, the vinyl version of that is far superior to the CD. Actually, the CD doesn't even sound like the vinyl version. I remember after recording it in the studio, and it sounded great. By that point, we were free agents in Europe, and we signed a deal with Chrysalis. So, I had the Chrysalis CD, and it didn't sound the same. It didn't have the excitement that was how it sounded in the studio.

It was about a year later, I was at someone's house who had a stereo and vinyl, and I listened to it, and it sounded great. It sounded just the way I remember it sounding in the studio. You really hear it on "Miracles."

**MARKY:** I thought the production was kind of iffy. If I had it my way, I would have made it fuller sounding. It's kind of mid-range, mid-rangey. But it came out okay. It was good to be asked by the people involved with [the film] *Pet Sematary* to do that song to it.

*How did that come about?*

**JOHNNY:** You'd have to ask Gary Kurfurst on that, probably. Gary's friends with Mary Lambert or was friends with Mary Lambert. Mary Lambert's the director and…I don't know. I don't know if Stephen King had anything to do with this or not. I don't really know what the story is.

**MARKY:** Well, Stephen King was always, is, will be, I guess, always a fan of the Ramones, and I guess Dee Dee got the book and that's how he wrote the song. He read the book. And then from there he got the song out of that. And then one thing led to another and then they chose that to do it. We went to Stephen King's house, I think it was '81, '82, maybe '83. That was a weird experience.

**JOEY:** Well actually, Stephen King is a big Ramones fan. He would mention us in all his books, little fill-ins about people checking into hotels under "Dee Dee Ramone, " this or that, mentioning song titles in the books and stuff. For years, every time he'd have a book release party in New York, he'd try to get ahold of us, and we'd always be on the road somewhere. So, eventually he really wanted to hook up with us, so he promoted a concert in Bangor, Maine, which is his home, and it was the Ramones and Cheap Trick. And so that way we could finally hook up together. So, after the show we met him, and he invited us for dinner and then over to his house, and it was really exciting. I remember he didn't invite Cheap Trick and they were kind of upset about that [laughs]. It was great. I remember, I think he had a bigger kitchen than Phil Spector, even.

JOHNNY: Yeah, Stephen King's a fan, but I don't think—Stephen King at that point sold the rights of the book to some movie company, right? He's not deciding who's in the movie and who does the soundtrack. I presume it just came down to that our manager was friends with the director and that got us the title song.

JOEY: Dee Dee wrote "Pet Sematary." He wrote it after readin' the book. And we shot a video for it with Bill Fishman. We shot it at the same cemetery, what's that guy? It's a real famous cemetery up in New York State. The headless horseman?

*"The Legend of Sleepy Hollow"?*

JOEY: The writer who did "Sleepy Hollow"?

*Washington Irving?*

JOEY: Yeah. I remember when we shot it, we were buried alive. It was an actual grave. And I remember it was a full moon, and it was pretty scary havin' to be buried alive a few times [laughs]. And I remember, I think the fact that we were there was kinda sacrilegious because the equipment truck caught fire on the highway after taking the equipment and like melted on the highway or something. It was kinda weird, kinda spooky.

*Brain Drain also featured Marky's songwriting debut with "Learn to Listen," cowritten with Dee Dee, Johnny, and Daniel Rey.*

**MARKY:** Yeah. Yeah. I can start with what happened was, at that point, a lot of times people would talk to me and I would not absorb what they were saying. I would let it go in one ear and out the other. And I thought that that was bad because it makes you stagnate. You don't learn, you don't grow. You don't try to better yourself.

It was basically something that I swished it around a little bit and then I made a go on the words. You know, if you don't listen sometimes, you're not going to become a better drummer or a better guitar player or a better songwriter. You're just going to be self-centered, and you'll only think that what you're doing is what matters. And that's not true because to keep your ears open you can learn a lot.

*At this point, Dee Dee suddenly leaves the Ramones. This is something that no band that's been around for a while wants to go through, to abruptly lose a founding member and a principal songwriter.*

**JOHNNY:** And a key member.

*How do you deal with that? How does a band go on from that point?*

**JOEY:** It was an emotional thing, and it came about without [warning]. Dee Dee just quit with no forewarning. And he kind of left to pursue his career as a rap singer, which is kind of amusing. And he put out that record "Funky Man" and *Standing in the Spotlight* and all that.

**MARKY:** He wanted to leave because he wanted to do a rap album. He's no rap artist, he's a rock artist. There's better people playing rap, but there's not anyone near where we come that are playing better than what we do with what we do. So, he did a [rap record] as a Ramone in the Ramones. There are better people like Run DMC that are doing better than him. There are other rap artists. It's too bad because he was my main friend in the group at the time. I'll always be his friend. I'll always respect what he is and his songwriting.

That was a pretty big blow to me. Like, what happened was I came back in '87 then he left in '89. So, for the two years that he was in the band, that we were together at that point, it was good being back friendly with him. And then when he left, I felt that I lost a friend. But we're still friends and everything is okay. It was shocking that that happened. He's the main songwriter.

**JOEY:** Well, at first, it was a shock [laughs], you know what I mean? But we persevered. And actually, that's when I had mentioned to this bass player that I knew, I asked them if they knew anybody. Actually, C. J. came from that. He was the first one.

**JOHNNY:** It was rough. Right away, I had everybody around me all saying, "Well, you better stop doing it now, you've gotta stop doing it now." And I go, "You're crazy, there's nothing to this. I'm gonna find somebody, I'll find a young Dee Dee, and it's not gonna be no problem at all and it's not gonna deter us in any way." Totally optimistic about the whole thing. But everybody was saying it to me, you know? [laughs] I thought there'd be no problem at all. I was being naïve about it, but the first person to come down to try out was C. J. And right away, just like I thought, there's gonna be no problem at all. This guy's good already; we'll just keep trying 'em out, there's gonna be a million Dee Dees coming in here, young Dee Dees. We tried about seventy-five more people, they were all horrible [laughs].

**MARKY:** And, of course, you got to go through everybody because the people find out about it and they work hard at it and you have to give them a chance.

**JOEY:** But when C. J. came down, he kinda had it. He kind of had what we were looking for. He seemed kinda cool. He was kind of like a young Dee Dee, I guess. He had the right attitude and the look.

**C. J. RAMONE:** I heard about the Ramones when I was kind of young because I was born in Queens, and I moved away eventually.

But I had some cousins that lived in Queens who were like real big on music and so I got turned on to them when I was real young. I didn't become a fan immediately, you know, because I was so young, but I was probably like about twelve or thirteen when I first heard of them.

*That's still pretty early in the Ramones' career, as far as that goes.*

**C. J.:** Definitely.

*Do you have any early favorites in the catalog—albums or songs?*

**C. J.:** Probably *Rocket to Russia* is my favorite.

*Did you like the* Rock 'n' Roll High School *movie?*

**C. J.:** To tell you the truth, I didn't really get it when I first saw it. It just seemed ridiculous to me. I didn't get the joke at all. Of course, later on, I got it. It's kind of funny because I always understood the Ramones' music and I got a real kick out of the jokes in their songs and stuff, but *Rock 'n' Roll High School*, I just could not grasp for some reason. I guess it's because when it comes to movies, my taste is more like science fiction.

*Would you want to do a movie with the Ramones?*

**C. J.:** I don't know if I would like to do a movie with the Ramones. I would like to act. I would like to try acting. A movie with the Ramones, though, would be a bit too nostalgic.

*Had you been in any bands before the Ramones? I know you came from the Marines into the Ramones. Had you been playing in any bands locally or anywhere?*

**C. J.:** For a little while I was playing with a band in New York City called Sweet Uranium.

*When would this have been?*

**C. J.:** This was in between the Marines and the Ramones. When I was younger, I played with a couple of heavy metal bands and stuff like that. Nothing really worth mentioning, though.

*How did you become a Ramone? How did that come about?*

**C. J.:** A friend of mine who played in a band with Joey's brother called up another friend of mine and told him about it. They told me, yeah, the Ramones are auditioning bass players. If you want to audition, you got to be at the studio by like six, so this is like…they called me at like three, you know? I live like two hours from the city in rush hour traffic. So, it didn't give me much time, but I figured out a couple of songs and jumped in my truck and took a ride to the city. I was the first one to audition, too, which was kind of neat. And I guess I must have auditioned a couple of times over the course of a month or two. And they ended up taking me.

**JOEY:** I guess with him, his story was that he went AWOL. He was in the Marines, and he heard that we were looking for a bass player and he came down to audition, and when he was accepted, he had to go get a passport and then the government got wind of his social security number and where he could be located. They came and picked him up and took him away to the brig.

And we waited for him.

**C. J.:** Yeah, yeah, yeah. After I auditioned a few times and I thought I would be getting a gig, I tried getting a discharge from the Marines 'cause that is what I had been waiting on, but I don't think they ever planned on giving me one. When I called them to find out the details, they ended up sending the cops to my house. I was arrested and ended up doing almost a month in the brig in Quantico, Virginia, right across from the FBI training headquarters.

**JOHNNY:** C. J. gets arrested for being AWOL from the Marines, and now I started getting concerned and worried. And then C. J. gets out of the [Marines]—God was looking after us. He said, "Well, I've given the Ramones a hard enough time, I'll give 'em a break." [laughs] So, C. J. comes out, and C. J.'s great.

**C. J.:** I know Johnny liked me from the start, you know. I think he was the one who was pushing to get me into the band. I don't know about Marky and Joey. From what I understand, Johnny was the only one who really thought I had what it took.

**JOEY:** And actually, C. J. coming into the band at the time, it was fresh blood, new blood, and he brought a new excitement into the band.

*He seemed to revitalize the band to some degree.*

**JOEY:** He did revitalize the band. Because there was a lot of infighting, there's always been a lot of bullshit in the band between me and John and stuff. But having him in the band just kind of made everything better all around. It was kind of a revitalization. It was great. I feel like since he's entered the band, the band's never been more exciting than it is right now. I mean, he takes it a step further than Dee Dee. And Dee Dee was an original, but it was refreshing having him in. And the band's stronger, and it became more fun and more exciting than before. With Dee Dee at the end there, it started becoming a bit stale and it wouldn't have lasted that much longer. It wasn't really a whole lot of fun anymore, and with C. J. in the band, it was kind of like a shot in the arm. And actually, it was more fun than I had remembered it being.

**C.J.:** It's a big compliment, but the way I look at it is that anybody that would have come into the band would have revitalized the band. I don't know if it would have been as much, or it could have been more. I just stepped into a situation where the band really needed a change. They've been doing it for so many years, for so long doing the same thing, and when Dee Dee left, that was their chance for a big change. I don't know if it really had so much to do with me as just the idea of somebody new and excited, somebody happy to be there back in the band.

*C. J., how did it feel to step into Dee Dee's shoes at this point? Here you are, noticeably younger than the rest of the band, and you get to replace someone who was an original member and one of the main songwriters.*

**C. J.:** To tell you the truth, I never thought of it that way. I approached it like I approach any job I took in my life. I got hired to do a job and I just did it the best that I could. You know, I had to take a lot of shit in the beginning, a lot of booing and Dee Dee chants and getting hit with stuff. I didn't just shy away from it. I just got out front and gave it right back to them. So, I eventually earned my place in the band.

**JOHNNY:** Have you seen him play yet, or what?

*Yeah, I saw him on the Escape From New York tour, the only chance I've had to see the new band.*

**JOHNNY:** C. J., try to see him again. He sings Dee Dee's songs great, and then he sings his own stuff. He's good. Now, all the new fans only really remember C. J.. Years ago, you used to hear about Tommy—now that doesn't mean anything.

**C. J.:** I think Dee Dee leaving was a much bigger thing, though, because he'll always be a Ramone. To me, Dee Dee was *the* Ramone. A lot of people think Joey and Johnny might be, but Dee Dee was like THE Ramone to me. Now that I am in the band, though, I see how things run and stuff, and I hear all the stories, I realize more that it's, in my opinion, Johnny who's been the driving force behind the band as far as keeping the band together and keeping it going. He's kind of the motivator. Dee Dee was definitely the songwriter and a big personality.

I know that back a couple of years ago, when I was a fan, I read a pretty funny thing in the paper about Marky had left the band and Richie was coming in and the guy made a statement to the effect of, "I wonder where they keep coming up with all these relatives that play instruments." I kind of laughed about it because, I mean, to this day people still think that there are brothers in the band.

Now that I am comfortable with my position, when I think about it, it *is* weird. Think of someone you really admire in the music business and then imagine taking their place in a band. It's a hard thing to relate to, but it is strange. It definitely is strange. The one song that we used to do live that I really felt strange doing was "Love Kills," because Dee Dee wrote this song about his own personal experiences with this chick Nancy [Spungen, the woman allegedly murdered by Sid Vicious]. I mean, I love this song. It's my favorite Ramones song, but I really felt weird singing it.

*Around this time, Sire began reissuing your first four albums as a pair of two-in-one CDs under the series title* All the Stuff (And More).

**JOEY:** Howie Klein, we had a meeting with him, and it was his idea for putting out dual CDs with additional bonus tracks. Which was kind of an exciting thing, ya know? I mean, we wanted it to be the individual artwork, we weren't really crazy about the fact that it didn't have that. But I think it came out well. And it was fun having the bonus tracks. And then there was *Volume Two*, with *Rocket to Russia* and *Road to Ruin*. I mean, it's really a great double.

**JOHNNY:** I prefer them as individual albums. It wasn't my idea, and now the next five unreleased ones, the middle period here, are all coming out as individual ones. We had no say—it was Sire doing it. We kept requesting single ones. I'd say, "What's the point of doing a cover if the cover's [not going to be used]?"

**JOEY:** I guess, earlier on, which we didn't mention, but I guess it was before doing the Phil Spector thing. Actually, we were in LA at

Gold Star and a friend of ours, Rodney Bingenheimer, was doing this project where he wanted—he had done one with Debbie Harry, what was the name of that....

*"Little GTO?" Rodney and the Brunettes.*

**JOEY:** Right, under an assumed name. He wanted to do one with us, where he wanted us to do "Surfin' Safari." So, we did it, and also at that session recorded "Slug," a song that I had written. And the producers were Phil Spector's bodyguards, the Kessel brothers, the sons of [jazz musician] Barney Kessel. After that session, we went to Phil's house. That was the first time we met Phil Spector, and that was quite an experience. So, I remember "Surfin' Safari" sounding great, but the master was lost. And I guess also they had done, when they put it together, they had the Honeys on it—you know, the Beach Boys' wives—and a bunch of different people, so it didn't really sound like us anymore. Because for one of the bonus tracks, [we] considered that track, but it didn't really sound like the Ramones anymore. So "Slug" went on [instead].

*Sounds like fodder for a Ramones* Odds and Sods *collection.*

**JOHNNY:** No, I hope not.

*Oh.*

**JOHNNY:** [laughs] The real collectors will find it anyway. Most of that stuff was not put out because it sucked.

**JOEY:** Yeah, there's a bunch of stuff that hasn't [been released]. I mean, there's kind of hopefully plans for something like that, you know, B-sides that didn't come out in America, you know. There's a bunch of things, a lot of early demos, there's a lot of demos that it would be great to finally be able to release. That would be great. Because I know myself, with a favorite artist, whether it be the Who or Bowie or whatever, that's always exciting.

We just got back from Japan, and I found this store there in Tokyo that, it's all like rock 'n' roll video, like real rare stuff. The whole store is just rock 'n' roll video, and everybody, they had VCRs so you could check out the quality of it. I found some amazing stuff, some real early Who from like '66, early Bowie from like '72, and it's just amazing stuff. Like Hendrix and all the stuff. So, it's pretty exciting.

*Your final album for Sire was* Loco Live, *another live album, and actually C. J.'s first record with the Ramones.*

**C. J.:** Right.

**MARKY:** That's right. The *Loco Live* we did in Spain. We were originally going to do it in Australia, but the mobile unit truck broke down and so we said we'd do it the next time we play.

**JOEY:** We were hoping all year to be able to find a spot. I remember initially when we were in Australia last year—actually it was three years ago—we were going to be doing a live radio broadcast. And the truck broke down, so it never came together. It was kind of a shame; it was a great show. But while we were out in Spain, we'd be going to Barcelona and there was a truck available. And the guy who owned the truck had spent time in New York and was a fan of the band. So, we got to use the mobile unit to tape the show in Barcelona, Spain. And that became *Loco Live*.

**JOHNNY:** I'm happier with *It's Alive!* We got some producer that the office found us that didn't know anything about the Ramones at all. I'm just not happy with it. I don't really know what's wrong with it, it's just not right.

**MARKY:** It was a very energetic album, a lot of energy in that album. I can't compare it to the Ramones' *It's Alive!* They're two different albums, but to me I liked the production on *It's Alive!* better than *Loco Live*, but I liked the energy on *Loco Live* better than *It's Alive!*

**JOEY:** I think it was a fun record, but to me the definitive [live] Ramones album is *It's Alive!*

*Loco Live may be best noted for returning "Carbona Not Glue" to retail shelves, albeit unbilled.*

**JOEY:** Right. We snuck it in because it was our last record for Sire, and we really wanted people to kinda get to hear it.

**JOHNNY:** Yeah, we snuck that in. We tried to get in other things, but they always tore it off. But that time we just put it down and put it in there—they don't even know about it [laughs].

*What was it like to leave Sire after all that time?*

**JOHNNY:** Oh, it was weird. Sire has always been nice to us. They wouldn't promote the records or anything, but I can't blame them.

**JOEY:** Yeah, well we felt that Sire really wasn't there for us, ya know? They weren't really there for us anymore, and actually not for some time. You know, they were putting all of their energies into Madonna and Depeche Mode and all that crap [laughs]. Ah, whatever....

**C. J.:** We were having, I think, problems on deciding on what was really going to happen. There were votes to stay with Sire but, in the end, I think everybody thought it would be best for the band. I don't think the record companies felt that way. They knew we were good for X amount of dollars without putting any money into us and anything. I believe they took us for granted. They took the band for granted a long time before I was with the band, too.

**MARKY:** Sire was great in the beginning but then, after a while, you [had] Madonna to deal with. I didn't even want to be a part of that anymore. I can't stand that shit. 'Scuse the language.

Some bad shit. I just hate it all. I was glad that I got off there because I just didn't want to be around it. It had nothing to do with what I thought anyways, but I was glad they were getting off to a more modernized label, something that wouldn't deal with that kind of stuff.

*From Sire to a new label, Radioactive. Radioactive is headed by your manager, Gary Kurfirst. Neat little package, that.*

**JOEY:** There was something exciting about the idea of your manager being the head of your label as well, kind of having a close-knit family ties. Some people told us, "Oh, it could be a conflict of interest." There are, at times. But at the same time, it is pretty exciting having it all in one place.

**JOHNNY:** Whew! I mean, you can discuss with your manager about promoting the record and go right to the source here. It makes it easier, instead of having to call your manager and complain to him about what the record company is doing, and then he calls the record company. So, it's all in one. It didn't have much of an effect, really, because we put [*Mondo Bizarro*] out and basically, I think it probably sold about the same as what we were selling [before].

**JOEY:** In a lot of ways, I felt like Radioactive was kind of like what Sire used to be when it was fresh and innovative. And here was a new company, it was being on the ground floor of something fresh and exciting and new.

And I remember, well, I changed my lifestyle by that point. I gave up alcohol and things like that. Actually, I was feeling really inspired in a way, I hadn't felt quite that inspired in a lot of years. The fact that Dee Dee wasn't in the band no longer, and, I guess I wanted to make a great album, like, I wanted to prove myself as well. I just wanted to have fun and make a great record.

*That record was* Mondo Bizarro. *Dee Dee even contributed some new songs.*

**JOHNNY:** Dee Dee wrote a couple of songs for the album. To me, probably the best song from the album, "Strength to Endure," and "Main Man," and—what was the other one?—oh, "Poison Heart."

**JOEY:** Yeah. Well, since [Dee Dee left the band], everything is cool with us and Dee Dee these days. You know, we all get along. And Dee Dee's going to be a contributor for the future.

Dee Dee, at that point, was looking to sell his songs, you know, that's what he was doing. So, we listened to a bunch of things, and we really liked "Poison Heart," [which] I thought was great, and "Main Man" and "Strength to Endure" were, like, really strong.

And I had written, like, seven other songs, and Marc contributed two, which was his first time kind of as a writer. Well, actually he had cowritten "Learn to Listen" on *Brain Drain*, with Dee Dee. It was an exciting time, you know, it's like a new album, ya know, and it's like the way things are with C. J. in the band and the whole bit. It was kind of exciting; it was very exciting. The album came out great. And Ed came back in, he really wanted to work with us again. It was kind of like a big family reunion.

**MARKY:** I'm real happy with the way that came out, the production. Of course, Ed had a lot to do with it. I wrote two songs on there. Not only that, it's just that the quality of, the feel of the album is real good, the song selection, the vibe was real cool. And that was done in New York, it was done in the early spring of '92, I think.

**C. J.:** I'm not real big on the studio, you know. I did my bass tracks and my vocal tracks in a total of probably about six hours or eight hours. I left the studio and never went back. I didn't hear the tape until about two weeks before the record came out.

I think it turned out pretty well. It's probably one of the best albums that came out since *Too Tough to Die*.

**JOHNNY:** It's not as good as *Too Tough to Die*, but it's good. At this point in your career, it's a very good album. It was good working with Ed, but you know, he changed his ways a little bit as far as recording. It's a little bit more, I guess, a new way of doing things, even though there's nothing wrong with the old way. I like the way the old albums sound, but all of a sudden now, it's like every piece together, every little thing. I really don't like working like that, but what can you do?

*Times change and Ramones change with them.*

**JOHNNY:** Well, yeah, I don't like that. I like times change and Ramones stay the same.

*Part of the Ramones' charm, I think. Although it's not true that all Ramones songs sound the same. That's no more true about you than it is about the Dave Clark Five or any other classic rock band—I hate to use the phrase.*

**JOHNNY:** I always thought we had a lot of variety. I don't know why they always say that, but I'm used to them saying it.

*It's an easy thing to say.*

**JOHNNY:** Though, sometimes I'm in the studio, and I'm listening to the instrumental track, and I go, "What song is this?" And I go, "I can't tell them apart without the words [laughs]." All the stuff sounds the same.

*C. J., you got to sing two songs on* Mondo Bizarro. *Had you been doing any singing before the Ramones?*

**C. J.:** No. I never sang in my life before this. I'm really not comfortable with singing. I don't really see myself as a singer. It's hard for me to…

*For someone who's not comfortable with singing, you seem to perform pretty well. Getting ahead of myself for a second, on* Acid Eaters, *you have three lead vocals. I think that is more than Dee Dee ever managed on a single album.*

**C.J.:** The most songs that Joey ever gave up on a record.

*The group dug up "Touring" for* Mondo Bizarro. *That was a song you'd had for a while—the Mystics recorded it in 1982 as "Doreen is Never Boring"—but this is the first time we've heard the Ramones' version.*

**JOEY:** I had written it for *Pleasant Dreams*, and actually, we did a version of it [for] *Pleasant Dreams*. I had written it around the time of "Sheena" and "Rock 'n' Roll High School," and Seymour felt it sounded too close to, I think, "Rock 'n' Roll High School," which it might've [laughs].

But it was a fun song. I mean, it really kind of conjures up all the great moments of why you're doing what you're doing. And from touring around the world and meeting all kinds of guys and girls [laughs], the whole bit. It was a fun song, a fun song to write.

*"Censorshit" stands alongside "Bonzo Goes to Bitburg" as one of the most overtly political tracks the Ramones ever did.*

**JOEY:** Yeah, well "Censorshit" dealt with record labeling and censoring of artists. And it was a lot of heavy stuff going on at that point, with the Moral Majority and the right-wing extremists. I mean, we were under attack, our civil rights were under attack, our human rights were under attack. And I felt very strongly about writing that.

And it was written as an open letter to Tipper Gore, who at the time was Senator Al Gore's wife. It was almost ironic when he was asked to be vice president. At first, I wasn't crazy about the idea at all. But actually, when I heard Al Gore speak in the vice presidential debate, I was very impressed by it. He's very sharp. And I think it was Hillary that told Tipper that if she didn't watch it, she was gonna knock her out, beat the shit out of her.

Also, one thing I thought was very cool about Gary and Radioactive was keeping the title, "Censorshit," which is exactly what it is. No asterisk or any of that shit.

*And you got to sing that very song on* The Tonight Show, *of all things.*

**JOEY:** Well, I thought that would be the ultimate slap in the face. It was perfect.

*I'm not sure if this is attributable to being on a new label or what, but it seems as though the Ramones are now enjoying a higher profile than you've had in years.*

**JOHNNY:** It seems like that. I'm never really sure. It seems like, you know, you hear about us all the time now.

**C. J.:** I don't know if it has anything to do with the new record company. It's possible, because we were the biggest asset that our record company really had when it first started, so that could have something to do with it. You know that it probably has a lot to do with our publicist, too, and not working and stuff like that. It's all business. That's what it all comes down to. It's just all business.

**JOEY:** Well, not to say anything derogatory about Seymour. I mean, I always thought Seymour was kind of a rebel, as well. But with Gary, it's in the true spirit of rock 'n' roll, a rebellious form. I mean, that's what rock 'n' roll always was, and today you'd never know it. But the Ramones retain the essence and the spirit of what it's all about.

*How did the Ramones' appearance on* The Simpsons *come about?*

**MARKY:** The guy who runs the show, or who is in charge of the show, is a fan. He wanted a song, so he found out that we were in New York, and he came down to the studio and asked us to say a few lines. So, we said our lines and he recorded them. He took some photos back, and they worked on the photos on how supposedly we looked to the artist there. And that's how we got on the show. We sang "Happy Birthday" to Mr. Burns.

*It's like the Standells appearing on* The Munsters. *It's a classic moment in TV history.*

**MARKY:** That was great. Do you remember *F Troop*? They had a thing with "Mr. Tambourine Man."

*Oh, yeah, yeah. I remember that.*

**MARKY:** That was wild. That was funny.

**JOHNNY:** I don't know who got it for us. They just did it, and we went to the studio on Fourteenth Street, said our lines, recorded "Happy Birthday." It took us longer to figure out how to play "Happy Birthday" than it did to record it. It became difficult to play because you only hear it a cappella. Took us a while to figure it out, fooling around with it for about half an hour or an hour, which is long.

**C.J.:** *The Simpsons* I wasn't surprised about. They have a lot of bands, like underground type bands on it, not even underground, like, you can't call the Chili Peppers and AC/DC underground, but you can call them, like, I don't know. I could just picture us being more on *The Simpsons* than I could on the Leno show, which we also did.

*Still, after all these years, the Ramones never appeared on* Saturday Night Live, *which I find amazing.*

**C. J.:** Isn't that incredible or what?

*It doesn't make any sense.*

**C. J.:** That's almost as bad as still not having a gold record.

*Yeah. I guess from what Joey was telling me,* Ramones Mania *is close.*

**C. J.:** Yeah.

*And probably will happen soon. I was on my way home tonight, and I stopped in a record store, and I mentioned that I was speaking to you tonight. And another guy was a customer there who just came up to say, "I never heard of the Ramones until eight months ago, and now the Rolling Stones are my second favorite band. I just love the Ramones.*

*They should come to Syracuse." See, you are winning new converts all the time. He picked up that Ramones book* [Ramones: An American Band *by Jim Bessman] that came out last year and saw about* Ramones Mania *almost going gold there. So, he went out promptly and did his part and bought a copy.*

**C. J.:** Ah. That's great.

**JOEY:** Well, again like so many other people, Matt Groening, he's a big Ramones fan. And he was really excited about trying to get us to appear on the show. And, I mean, I thought it was like one of the ultimate honors, because, I mean, he's a fuckin' genius and the show's great. I think it's like the best thing on television. I mean, it's just great quality television, and the fact that he can deal with so many different topical [concerns]. Oh, yeah, it's a riot, man. And it was a lot of fun doing what we did. And the show, I thought it was great. I still think it's one of the best episodes. It just has everything in it. Heartwarming [laughs].

**JOHNNY:** But it was an easy day's work, I mean, they did my line, recorded the song in about ten minutes and gave us a Simpsons coat and a union card, and paid us. So, it was a good day. I was home in about two hours [laughs].

*There you go! On* Mondo Bizarro, *a cover of the Doors' "Take It as It Comes" leads to a whole album of sixties covers,* Acid Eaters.

**JOHNNY:** First of all, on "Take It as It Comes," one day I was outside, and I just heard the song through a closed door or something, I heard it on a tape and I thought, "Wow! That song's for us." I come back and I suggest we should do a Doors song, "Take It as It Comes." And they go, like, "A Doors song? We shouldn't play no Doors song!" And I go, "No, this is the right song for us. I hear it as a Ramones song." And it came out good. A lot of covers I don't like when we do 'em, but that was a good one.

So then, last year, they wanted to release "Take It as It Comes" as a single for the summer, and they wanted to do an EP, and they said, "Why don't you record a couple of other songs?" I also wanted to…I chose "Take It as It Comes" because I wanted to get away from the period of the early sixties. Every time we chose a cover, we chose one from the early sixties. And even though "Take It as It Comes" is basically '65–'66, it's more identified with the Doors, [who] are a part of the later sixties and psychedelic era and everything else. Doors are a great group.

**JOEY:** Well, that was really how it all came about. "Take It as It Comes" was gonna be the second single from *Mondo Bizarro*, and Gary said, "Well, why don't you guys record five additional songs, and we'll make it, like, an EP, like a treat for the fans and all."

**C. J.:** I guess everybody just had a lot of fun doing that cover. And our manager decided that maybe it would be a good idea for us to do a covers album, so he put it to the band. I really wasn't for it. I thought it was a bit too nostalgic, kind of concentrating on a…something that could almost be detrimental to our image. It seems like people think of too much of the past when it comes to the Ramones. You hear so much of the Ramones' history and not enough about what's going on about the Ramones now. And I think that hurts them sometimes. And I thought that this album was just contributing to that. I still think it is. But at first it was supposed to be an EP, so I said, well, that ain't bad. We recorded some songs, we went away on tour, we came back, and our manager had, like, sold some of our shit. He decided that maybe we should do an album. So, after a while, I guess, I warmed up to the idea. I said, yeah, I guess it's okay. Now I feel like I did in the beginning, that maybe we should've waited 'til the summer and did a studio album. It was mostly our manager's idea. We wouldn't have done it if we didn't want to, put it that way. But it got enough votes to go through.

**JOHNNY:** So, they wanted to release an EP and "Take It as It Comes" as a single off of it, and they said, "Record some other oldies." I said, "I don't know about this. I don't want to be identified [as] doing a bunch of oldies. I don't wanna be locked in, just let me think about this for a few days." I mentioned it to a few friends and fans, and no one was being negative on it. I didn't wanna go if we were getting negative reactions from the fans on the streets. So, I said okay, fine with me.

So, we recorded a few songs, and it came out good. And they said, "Well, we're not gonna get a summer tour, no point putting this song out as a single. Why don't you just go ahead and do an album of it?" And at that point, it was sort of, like, fun trying to figure out what to do and try to interpret the songs and everything else. So, at that point it was fun, and I figured, "Ah, let's finish it."

**JOEY:** So, we did, and the songs really came out great. And we chose some of our favorite songs, songs that we felt that we could do really well. We went for more obscure favorites. And actually, one of the songs was "Substitute," and Pete Townshend came down and sang background vocals, which was a real highlight for me. 'Cause Townshend's a hero of mine. To me, I guess the Beatles and the Who for me were, like, my favorite bands. I'm sure I love the other bands, too, but those bands were special. You know, the Rolling Stones and the Kinks…I don't know. It was just Townshend, to me personally, was a real major inspiration as far as influencing the songwriter, and he's a great performer. In a lot of ways, I think the Ramones are closer to a band like the Who, you know what I mean? Because it's real and it's honest and it's exciting. I mean, everybody was a unique individual, and the band was so exciting, and they were loud [and] great.

**MARKY:** We always do a cover song on each of our albums, anyways. It's not really nothing new that we did *Acid Eaters*. But the response to it was real good. The people at Radioactive wanted us to do an EP, so instead of doing an EP, they liked what we had on the EP, so they wanted us to do an album. So, we did the album instead, and that was a lot of fun because I always liked those songs as singles growing up as a kid.

"7 and 7 Is" by Love was something totally off the wall when I heard it, the lead and the guitar playing on it. And the other stuff, you know, the other things that was on there. "My Back Pages" by Bob Dylan, but I liked the Byrds' version better. And "Have You Ever Seen the Rain," we used our style, the beat of our style to it. And it has a sixties production feel on the album. I liked the production because it's edgy and it isn't so perfect. Some productions are so perfect today that it's just so sterile sounding. Things are so sterile sounding that a lot of the time it sounds like a machine making the music. And that's why I like this sound, because it's edgy and raw.

**JOEY:** I think it came out great. We just came off a big tour of Australia and Japan, [did] a lot of in-stores, and when I hear it, I just think it sounds great. I think the production's perfectly suited for it, it's kinda that trash, kind of garagey feel. And the video [for "Substitute"] came out great, I think it's the best video we ever made, and I think we made a lot of great videos. We worked with this guy Tom Rainone, who's a good friend of John's. He's a director, he's done a lot of horror stuff. And it's kind of like an all-star cast, Lemmy and Lux [Interior, of the Cramps]. It's got that, well, I guess some of the most B-, exploitation film stars. And it has that feel, that kind of exploitation type of film feel. Yeah, the video came out great. It really has everything in it. It's fun, it's wild, it's sex, violence, rock 'n' roll, the whole bit, but well-intended.

*Done with wit and taste.*

**JOEY:** Yeah, you know, it's very clever. It's like a mini film. I really enjoyed making *Acid Eaters*. It was just a lot of fun to do, we did it really fast and the versions came out great for the most part. Actually, recently when I was in Japan, I met Bob Dylan, which was exciting.

I mean, because of *Acid Eaters* I've gotten to meet a bunch of people who were kinda heroes. And actually, I gave him a copy of it. I don't know what he thinks of it. But maybe I'll get some feedback at some point [laughs].

*This just occurs to me. At one point, Springsteen was supposedly writing a song for the Ramones. Was there any truth to that?*

**JOEY:** No, there was never any truth to it. He came to see us, like, years ago when we were playing at the Fast Lane in Asbury Park, New Jersey. Him and Little Steven came. *[NOTE: Apparently Springsteen was going to give his song "Hungry Heart" to the Ramones, but Bruce's manager told him he was crazy and to keep the song for himself. In 1980, "Hungry Heart" became Springsteen's first-ever Top 10 single.]*

*How did you pick the songs for* Acid Eaters?

**JOEY:** We went through our collections, and we tossed ideas around, and for the most part, like "7 and 7 Is" and "Can't Control Myself," "Can't Seem to Make You Mine," most of them were all our favorites. "Somebody to Love" was suggested by our manager. But for me, I thought it was kind of a challenge. We otherwise wouldn't have done a song like that. But Traci Lords, she's also our label mate, to find the right song [for her to sing backup], that was chosen. And I don't know, whatever.

**JOHNNY:** Different people would suggest songs, and we'd say "No." It depends on the song. You'd have to go through each song probably. Basically, each day Marc and me and C. J. would be rehearsing for this, just us three. And C. J. wasn't familiar with any of these old songs, he heard them after we suggested them. Marc said one day, "Let's do '7 and 7 Is,' you wanna do '7 and 7 Is?'" I say, "Oh, great song! You think we can do it? Yeah, let's try it." So, me and C. J. learned the song. And I was amazed that we could play these songs. I said, "You wanna try a Bob Dylan song?," even though I don't like

Bob Dylan. I'm not a fan of Bob Dylan in any way. I think it would be funny to do a punk version of a Bob Dylan song. So, we did that like that, and had C. J. sing it.

*C.J. sings quite a bit more on this album.*

**JOHNNY:** Yeah, he had three songs on it. He was singing it all at rehearsal, because while we were doing it just with us three, he was singing everything. So, a lot of songs, I got used to hearing him sing the songs.

*C. J., not to harp too much with you being a little younger than the rest of the band, were you familiar with most of the songs in their original versions?*

**C. J.:** No. No. I hadn't heard most of them before. I wasn't familiar with them at all. Which kind of made figuring them out a bit interesting, because of the way I figured them out and I had to arrange a couple of them also. And not being familiar with them, it gave them a kind of a fresh, like new sound almost. Except for like "When I Was Young," that there ain't much you can do with.

*There's a nice piledriving through "My Back Pages."*

**C. J.:** That's great, isn't it?

*It's just terrific. I like the Byrds' version of it, but I think the Ramones' version stands up real well.*

**C. J.:** That's probably my favorite song on the record. That or "7 and 7 Is."

*Ah. That has always been a great song. Funny enough, I know that the Bangles were going to record a cover of that a few years back. I guess they never quite got around to doing that.*

**C. J.:** They were going to record "7 and 7 Is"?

*Yes, they were. I remember seeing them do it live, and they said it was going to be on their next album. This would have been '85 or so, I think. This was before they had any hits.*

**C. J.:** That's wild!

**JOHNNY:** We kept getting a lot of outside pressure from management of the record company, saying, "Why don't you do a song that we heard of, why don't you [do] this, why don't you do that?" And making ridiculous suggestions, "Why don't you do 'She's Not There'?" Go back and listen to the song; if you hear the Ramones doing this song, then come back and tell me about it again, you know? These people had no idea what they're talking about, and they just make off-the-wall suggestions.

*Any songs that you tried screwing around with that just didn't work out?*

**JOHNNY:** Probably a few that are on the album [laughs]. But at that point it was too late.

**JOEY:** Well, there's one song we did record and decided not to put it out. We did another version of "Surfin' Safari." And we didn't really like the way [it turned out]. Actually, it is out on the Japanese *Acid Eaters* CD. They stuck it on. I know initially C. J. was supposed to sing the Animals song ["When I Was Young"], but he couldn't quite get it. Actually, I was kinda happy to be able to sing that one.

**JOHNNY:** We were doing "Out of Time," and then thought I wasn't happy with the way it was sounding at rehearsal. Then I said, "Let's learn 'Sitting on a Fence.'" We learned "Sitting on a Fence," I wasn't happy with how that was sounding. It was sounding too country to me. So, I said, "Let's go back to 'Out of Time' again." Went back to "Out of Time," and I realized that at that point it was a song that was gonna have to be done in the studio with studio production. With us three playing it, it really wasn't getting the real effect of the recording. Came out good in the recording, though. A lot of songs we had to visualize what they were doing. [With] "When I Was Young," we would try to visualize what it was gonna sound like with all the other parts on. "Can't Seem to Make You Mine," with getting the right keyboard sound....

*Done by a group that could have been called the sixties Ramones, the Seeds. Sky Saxon even looked a little bit like Joey.*

JOHNNY: [laughs] And we kept getting a lot of flak from them not to do the Amboy Dukes song because they don't like Ted Nugent, they don't like the Amboy Dukes, don't do that song.

*That's like perfect Ramones fodder, too; it's a Ramones song to begin with.*

JOHNNY: Every day, he's calling me up, "You're not doing that song, are you?" And I finally started to say, "No, no, we're not doing it," so they wouldn't bother me. We just went in and did it, I didn't care. Now they love it, they put it [as] the first song on the album [laughs]. "Surf City" didn't come out good, I don't like "Somebody to Love," I don't like "Substitute." Different reasons on different songs. "Substitute," basically, it's not bad but I really don't like nothing about it. I'm not thrilled about the playing, I'm not thrilled with the singing, I'm not thrilled with Pete Townshend's singing, I'm not thrilled with the lead vocal. "Somebody to Love," another one like that where nothing is really...it's nobody's fault, it's just a difficult song to do. Really hard. Sometimes you can play a song so well, then even if the singing isn't what I pictured, the song will still be good, it'll still be okay. That one, it was just very hard to do. And then we were fooling around with those guitar sounds, trying to get that guitar sound that whatever his name is, Jorma....

*Jorma Kaukonen?*

JOHNNY: Yeah. The closer we could get to his sound on the overdub guitars, the more it clashed with my original rhythm tracks. It was hard, and Gracie Slick sings it so good [on the Jefferson Airplane version], that you can't compete. Plus, I had to think at the time they suggested Traci Lords singing on a song. You know, Traci's nice, and I'm trying to think of a song that the Ramones are gonna be able to do, and that's gonna be right for the Ramones and it has to be right for a girl singing on it. It was difficult to come up with something that was gonna be right.

*1994 marks the twentieth anniversary of the Ramones, and you also put on your 2,000th show in Japan this past February. How does one look back on twenty years of beating on the brat with a baseball bat? Twenty years later, what's it like to be a Ramone?*

**JOHNNY:** I hear that every day, "How does it feel to be a legend?" [laughs] How does it feel to be a legend, how does it feel to influence all these people, how does it feel to do this, everybody wants to know how we feel. Everyone compliments you everywhere you go. It's weird [laughs].

**JOEY:** We're gonna be on tour all year. In April, Sire's releasing those five CDs that previously haven't been [reissued]. Also, *Ramones Mania* is just about turning gold. It's funny, because I've had mixed feelings over the years and months and stuff, but actually having accomplished 2,000 performances in twenty years with my fellow bandmates...! I mean, I kind of looked at it kind of trivially, but having accomplished it, it really is a major feat.

First of all, there aren't many bands who have actually done 2,000 performances—maybe the Grateful Dead, maybe—but also working close, a very close-knit situation, constantly touring, it's very, very difficult.

*But touring is never boring.*

**JOEY:** Touring is never boring, not in this band. Never a dull moment. But the realization, it's been a feat to do this.

**MARKY:** When I first heard the band, *Ramones*, the album, I was with Wayne County, and we were hanging out upstairs in Max's and he was the DJ and he played the album and I said, "What the fuck is this?" Then I listened to it again and I said, "This is the start of something new." For me to say that, after a life learning Beatles stuff and playing to Keith Moon and Jimi Hendrix, it was hard for me now to realize that I said it because I really felt it. And I said to myself, I wonder if I'll ever be in a band like this that can create something like these guys are going to create.

They didn't even go to England yet. This was like, I think, April of '76, and they didn't even go to England to start that whole scene over there with [the British punks]. They were in the audience watching the band. They didn't even form yet. They formed a little later on, but they weren't around in '74 or '75. In England, it was all punk rock, so getting back to hearing them for the first time, it amazed me because the production sucked on it, but there was something there that was a surge of power, energy. It didn't mean that you had to play lead guitar for ten minutes. It didn't mean that you had to do a powerful drum solo. As a unit, there was no spaces in the structure of the songs. There was such a barrage of eighth notes that there was no spaces. It was like a train. It was like being in a train station or hearing a jet take off. It was a combination of those two things. Then the next thing I knew, after playing with Richard Hell, they asked me to play with them. I was very happy for that.

*Be careful of what you wish for....*

**MARKY:** Ah, yeah, definitely.

**JOEY:** I guess one of the highlights was when *Spin* magazine named us [as one of the seven most important bands ever]. That was something that came out of the blue for me. I know that we've affected everybody, without sounding modest or anything, but it's true. I mean, I think rock 'n' roll is healthier because of the Ramones. I remember in the eighties going through all these different phases, techno pop and all this shit, and now at least everything's back to basics; it's kind of back to free expression and being adventurous, and that's great.

**C. J.:** What I usually say is it's just like a dream. When you're young and you're sitting around and you listen to bands, and you would, like, give anything to be in a band, in *that* band you think about. When I was younger, I had a fantasy of going to a concert of a favorite band and something happened to the bass player and I got to go on stage and play with them.

*Sure.*

**C. J.:** It's kind of what it's like. It's like a dream but when you get there...! When I got there, there was just so much work involved, and getting used to being on the road and getting used to signing autographs and not being Chris Ward anymore, being C. J. Ramone, it was such a big transition I never really had a chance to sit back and think about it and say, "Wow!" I mean, there were times I was on stage, and I would be playing, and I'd look to my right and see Johnny and Joey and think to myself, "Holy shit, this is unbelievable that I'm up here playing with these guys." And it's such a great feeling, but then there's those nights when you have an argument before you go on stage and you look over and you're thinking to yourself, "This ain't worth it."

*Any plans for the next twenty years?*

**MARKY:** I'm sure Keith Richards, when the Stones approached their twentieth anniversary, he didn't feel the band would go on to their thirtieth year. And they've been together for thirty-two years. I don't know if we can achieve that, and I don't know if we want to do that. But if it happens that we are together for another two or three years, that would be fine with me.

**JOHNNY:** No, probably do another studio album later in the year. Dee Dee's already written a whole bunch of songs—that's good.

I heard about ten songs he'd written; I think we chose six of them that I was interested in. I don't know. I mean, I just think about one year at a time. I don't know, the time is gonna come to stop soon. I don't wanna become a joke, and I don't wanna be not as good. You have to stop at some point. No one ever stops, though.

*It's the thing, like the Beatles or the Stones saying, "I can't see doing this when I'm thirty, for God's sake." But real life catches up I guess, and you find that you can still do it at thirty or forty. Keith Richards is always saying how it will be interesting to see if we can still do this into our sixties like the blues guys do.*

**JOHNNY:** No, I'm not doing it. I'm stopping soon, I just don't know when. I mean, it's hard to tell. You never know when all of a sudden, an album does well for some miracle or something like that. But I don't know. I'd like to do another album. I don't know beyond that. I don't know.

**JOEY:** We have been at the Rock and Roll Hall of Fame that they're putting together. They're gonna have a permanent Ramones kind of archive there. That was pretty cool. I feel like we haven't gotten our justification, so little things like this kind of make up for it. You know, like *The Simpsons* and this and that, just make it great. It's fun.

**JOHNNY:** That seems to be happening a little bit now. We've been getting a lot of recognition lately, you know? It's a weird feeling. I don't know, I don't know. To me, I always feel like after you're done playing, you're sort of like forgotten. But I don't know.

*My wife likes to compare the Ramones to the Grateful Dead, in terms of just a band that is phenomenally popular on one level but doesn't sell a lot of records.*

**JOHNNY:** I've heard that a lot. I'm not a fan of the Grateful Dead, but I keep getting that comparison. I mean, I'm not a fan of them at all [laughs]. But Jim Bessman mentioned that a few times in his book.

*It's a comparison that doesn't go away, even though the styles of music obviously aren't the same.*

**JOHNNY:** Well, the Grateful Dead—I don't even look at them as any sort of influence on anyone, though. I know they're off in their own little world, and we're off in our own world, and we've played 2,000 shows, the Grateful Dead are probably around that number, too. You know, [for] the cult type band, that record sales are sort of limited. But I just don't feel like they were an influence on...I can't look back and say that the Grateful Dead are one of the great bands of rock 'n' roll.

*I'm not sure that they'd even be called a rock 'n' roll band. I don't mind them, personally, but they're not what I envision when I say the phrase "rock 'n' roll." The Kinks would come to mind. The Ramones would come to mind.*

**JOHNNY:** Yeah. I mean, there are a couple of similarities. They wouldn't go away either.

*Final question: How does it feel, after twenty years, to be a Ramone? Is it something that you look back on with some pride?*

**JOHNNY:** Oh, yeah, yeah! I enjoy it more now than probably ever, but I know I have to stop at some point. In the beginning, you're doing it, you don't really look back. When you're toward the end of your career, which you have to be after a twenty-year mark—you can't be in the middle of it, you're toward the end—I've been really blessed that I've been able to do this for twenty years, and that so many people are so nice to me everywhere I go. I've been really lucky; I've been very fortunate.

*Looking back, can you pick out favorites, either songs or whole albums? Johnny mentioned* Rocket to Russia *as his favorite Ramones album. Are there other moments that stand out in a twenty-year career as a Ramone?*

**JOHNNY:** Other individual albums? *Too Tough to Die*, *Leave Home*, *Road to Ruin*—I'm happy with those.

Every album's got some songs I like, and every album's got some songs I don't like. Even on *Rocket to Russia* there's probably something on there that I don't like. You always want to make the album where you like every single song. It's impossible [laughs].

**JOEY:** I think, for me, there's just so many moments, especially with the albums. Each album has its own personal kind of signature, let's say. And I guess just writing songs and where they were written and how they came about, you know what I mean? I guess working with Phil Spector was kind of special; that was like nothing else, lemme tell you that [laughs]!

Each album really has its own place. It's really hard to pick. I guess some of my favorite albums, I'd say *Mondo Bizarro* is one of my favorite albums. I mean, it was a special time for me, a very inspiring and stimulating period, so that's definitely one of my favorites. The *Acid Eaters* came out great and it was a lot of fun to do, but *Mondo Bizarro* is kind of more special to me. And I remember *Too Tough to Die* was great. They all have something, but I guess like *Leave Home* and *Rocket to Russia*. I don't know.

*Johnny, if you had to do it over again, would you have been a Ramone or a New York Yankee?*

**JOHNNY:** Oh, boy! [laughs] That's tough, you know? I mean, if I could have had a twenty-year career as a Yankee, I probably would have been a Yankee. Not to have a five-year career, no, then I'm probably better off with this. But a twenty-year career with the Yankees? Boy, that'd be great. But this is pretty good, too.

**JOEY:** When you're doing it, it's great. When you're out there playing, it's great. It's still just as exciting as it ever was.

# I JUST WANT TO HAVE
# SOMETHING TO DO
*Additional comments from Joey Ramone*

*In this book's introduction, I mention receiving an unexpected phone call from Joey Ramone about a week after our initial interview. Although I wasn't prepared for the call and therefore wasn't ready to record it, I tried to take notes of what Joey said. I incorporated some of the material from those notes in the introduction, all the while wishing that I had a permanent record of the conversation.*

*There was never an audio record of that second phone call. But, while reviewing material for this collection, I was surprised to discover my original notes of that call. I did not think that transcript survived, but there it was, tacked on to the end of the transcription of my first interview with Joey. I can't guarantee that I scribbled down everything Joey said verbatim, but I betcha I came pretty close. Here's that transcript, preserved for posterity.*

## SECOND CALL

**JOEY:** When we were running down the events of the band, there were a couple of more records that weren't mentioned, and I didn't know if they should be. One was that I had done—I guess it was in '82—I did a single with Holly Vincent [of Holly and the Italians].

*Yeah, the Holly and Joey single?*

**JOEY:** Yeah. I've always been a real big fan of Holly's work. To me, she's like a genius. She's really unique in her ways. She's got a new

114

band called the Oblivious. She's got an album out now on a small label called Daemon, that's Relativity Records. Actually, I'd like to work with her in the future. She's got some great stuff that she never recorded that I've heard, and I'd like to work with her. In the future, I'd like to produce a couple of songs for her that I've heard. I've heard a lot of her demos and this and that, and she's great, she's a great songwriter. Matter of fact, the version that we did of "I Got You, Babe" and hearing that new version, the Beavis and Butthead version with Cher, I mean, the way the guitars are on that I feel kinda took a lot off the record we did.

*Many Ramones fans are probably barely aware of that single's existence. Certainly relatively few have heard it.*

**JOEY:** Well, some of them are because at record stores I see it. The thing is, it was on some CD but it sounded like shit. The actual single, the way it was mixed and all, was real great, it sounded real exciting. It was fun, and it was like a total spontaneous move. She was in London, I was in Spain, and we were talking, and we just did it, spur of the moment thing. I didn't even tell my manager [laughs].

And recently, I did a reworked version of "Rockaway Beach" that's kinda R & B-flavored with General Johnson [of soul group the Chairmen of the Board]. It was real exciting, because it was a whole new avenue. It was part of an album called *Godchildren of Soul*, but I don't know if that album will be coming out. But this single that we did together, I'm sure this will be showing up in the future, maybe in a soundtrack or something. But it's a really unique version, and it came out great.

*And you're on that* In Their Own Words *songwriters' disc on Razor & Tie, singing "I Wanna Be Sedated" with Andy Shernoff of the Dictators.*

**JOEY:** Also, [the Ramones] did a version of the Heartbreakers song "I Love You" for the Johnny Thunders tribute. Actually, it came out great. Daniel Rey produced it.

Actually, I did a duet with Debbie [Harry], I think I told you. It wasn't released yet. Debbie, when we did "Go Lil' Camaro Go," she came, and we did that. I guess about a year ago, when she was recording her new album, or her current album, Chris and Debbie called me and asked me if I would do a duet type of thing on this song called "Standing in My Way." So, I did it, and it was great to do. The bass player had written the song. The version that we did didn't appear on her album. I think in England it might have been released along with the album, ya know, you could acquire it if you wanted it. But it's going to be put out at some point. And it came out great.

Right now, I'm working on a project with my brother. His name is Mickey Leigh. Years back, he had a band called the Rattlers that a lot of people know about. He's done a lot of work throughout, working with different people. Like Lester Bangs, he had a band with him called Birdland. I guess he's had a few bands recently, a band named Tribe, and Crown the Good. But right now, he's got a new band. I always wanted to work with him because I think he's a really talented guy, a great songwriter, great guitar player, he's got a great style, real original and exciting. So, he's working with kind of a three-piece situation right now. His new songs, I think, are great, and so we decided to do a project together. We're gonna call it Sibling Rivalry, because that's how brothers are. It's a reworked version of Blodwyn Pig's "See My Way." It was a very obscure English band, and it's a great song, and he rearranged it and it's like much better than the original. So, we're gonna do the song, take different parts in the vocals. Daniel Rey's the producer, and it's comin' out great.

# WE'RE OUTTA HERE!
# AFTER THE BLITZKRIEG ENDS
*I Dream of Johnny, Joey, Dee Dee, Tommy (and occasionally Marky, Richie, C.J., and/or new recruits)*

I occasionally dream about the Ramones. It doesn't happen often, but it's happened a few times. In the dreams, they're still alive, still playing. Sometimes the personnel have changed, and there are newer Ramones in place of some veteran Ramones. As I dream, I don't know if I'm aware that Johnny, Joey, Dee Dee, and Tommy have all gone to that great Fifty-Third and Third in the sky. I generally don't dream of interacting with them; I'm just there, standing in the back at a crowded concert hall, enjoying the live sound of the group I call the American Beatles, the greatest American rock 'n' roll band of all time.

My most recent Ramones dream was different. I met Joey Ramone at a café. We sat and chatted at a little table, awaiting our drink orders. Joey was excited about a brand-new Ramones single. "This is gonna be a hit," he said, "This one's finally gonna be our hit single!"

Joey produced a Walkman or an iPod—you know how dreams are—and played the song for me. It was poppy and fast and catchy, like a Ramones record should be. But the vocals weren't what I expected. It definitely wasn't Joey singing.

I asked Joey, "Is that C. J.?" Joey's expression changed. "No," he said, a tinge of melancholy in his voice. "We got a girl singer now." He sighed, a saddened tone in his voice. "This is gonna be a hit."

I woke up. And I was sad, too.

# THE GREATEST RECORD
# EVER MADE!

*This entry was originally written for my book-in-development,* The Greatest Record Ever Made! (Volume 1), *but is not included in that work.*

*An infinite number of tracks can each be THE greatest record ever made, as long as they take turns. Today, this is THE GREATEST RECORD EVER MADE!*

**THE RAMONES: I Don't Want to Grow Up**
Written by Tom Waits and Kathleen Brennan
Produced by Daniel Rey
From the album *¡Adios Amigos!*, Radioactive Records, 1995

There would be no hit records. The road to ruin reached its predetermined end.

In 2002, *Spin* magazine ranked the Ramones second on its list of the fifty greatest bands of all time, with only the Beatles perched above them. Writer Marc Spitz explained the rationale of placing this seemingly misfit Carbona Quartet just a step below England's phenomenal pop combo:

"Punk rock exists because of the false assumption that the Ramones can be imitated. '1-2-3-4!' Three chords. 'Second verse, same as the first.' Technically speaking, it's simple. Legend has it that in every city where the Ramones played in support of their 1976 debut, a handful of punk kids started up bands, thinking that they could do it, too. But the Ramones' loud-fast style masked a pop genius. Slow their tempos, and you've got Beach Boys harmonies. Replace lyrics about sniffin' glue and eatin' refried beans, and you've got the Ronettes. Give everyone matching leather jackets, and you've got the punk-rock Beatles. Just four lads from Queens who birthed thousands of bands, then blew each one away."

I believe I may have dropped the magazine at that point just so I could give it a standing ovation.

We have not yet created a language that can adequately convey the sheer, visceral *thrill* of that precise second when I realized the Ramones were...*perfect.* Just perfect. Punk? Sure, yeah. Rock 'n' roll? Oh, *God*, yes. But also, power pop, bubblegum, every great song ever played on any AM radio ever conceived on Earth or above, all distilled into this massive, physical presence that's simultaneously as heavy as a truncheon and as light as helium candy. Pop music, played loud, played fast, and played for keeps, our hearts sustained by its velocity, our souls redeemed by its purity, our faith in the transcendent power of music restored by forceful melody, accomplished as easily as the above-cited count of 1-2-3-4.

And for all that, the Ramones never had a goddamned hit record. Not in America anyway. "Sheena Is a Punk Rocker" charted. "Rockaway Beach" made it all the way up to #66 in *Billboard*, and a cover of "Do You Wanna Dance" wrote *finis* to the Ramones' brief three-part invasion of the lower half of the Hot 100, all accomplished in 1977–78. Like the immortal "Blitzkrieg Bop" before it, "I Wanna Be Sedated" did not chart. "Do You Remember Rock 'n' Roll Radio?" did not chart. "Rock 'n' Roll High School" did not chart. Radio's ears were closed to the Ramones. Retail declared them niche, cult...*lesser.* MTV all but ignored them.

The Ramones pretended not to care. They insisted that hit records never mattered to them. Their practiced scowls feigned indifference to what the buying public thought of them, and hid the fact that they were lying through their teeth.

*Of course* the Ramones wanted hit records! They'd come of age in a time when the greatest records *were* hits, from Del Shannon to the Dixie Cups, James Brown to the Beatles. They never outgrew the quaint notion that the best stuff could be the most popular stuff, the most popular stuff the best stuff. They didn't want to grow up. They couldn't.

*When I'm lyin' in my bed at night*
*I don't want to grow up*
*Nothing ever seems to turn out right*
*And I don't want to grow up*

The Ramones' final studio album was 1995's *¡Adios Amigos!* Its stated intent to be the Ramones' farewell effort was tacitly understood to carry an asterisk: the final album* (*unless this one's a hit). It was not. But Jesus, it should have been.

The album opens with a supercharged Ramonesified reading of Tom Waits's "I Don't Want to Grow Up," a triumphant bludgeoning that plants its feet and establishes one last Rockaway Beachhead. There would be no hit records. That 2002 *Spin* piece concluded, "Like sharks, the Ramones never evolved. They didn't have to." Growin' up is for squares, man.

The Ramones weren't gonna do it.

We don't have to do it either.

# HERE TODAY, GONE TOMORROW
## Joey Ramone 1951–2001

*This reminiscence of Joey Ramone and what the Ramones meant to me appeared in* Yeah Yeah Yeah *magazine in 2001.*

The Ramones were the greatest (i.e., my favorite) American rock 'n' roll group of all time. They were second only to the Beatles in my personal pop pantheon, and I've taken recently to referring to them as "The American Beatles." And if that statement makes you roll your eyes or presume I'm kidding, then you're a cretin, plain and simple. Granted, the Ramones never came anywhere near the Beatles' massive record sales—if the Ramones were ever to issue a counterpart to the Beatles' *1*, they'd have to use a negative number—but they were just as important, just as invigorating, just as much the salvation of rock 'n' roll as that other Fab Four.

The passing of Joey Ramone was not a surprise—many people knew how sick he was, though few spoke of it—but the news of his death on Easter Sunday still hit hard, making my eyes sting and my teeth clench. I never met Joey (though I had the pleasure of doing a very lengthy telephone interview with him several years ago), but I still felt a sense of personal loss.

And it *is* a personal loss, really. My life would be at least a little bit different if not for the Ramones, and my view of music would be radically different. I've written elsewhere of how the Ramones' 45 of "Sheena Is a Punk Rocker" is the one record that changed my life, the magical track that opened my eyes and ears to a new sense of how great and transcendent rock 'n' roll could be in the (then-) here and now, not just in the Beatle-occupied past.

This wasn't the first time I'd heard the Ramones—I'd been requesting selections from their debut LP for play on my college radio station, and was already becoming a fan—but when I bought that single out of curiosity and finally let it play, I was hooked, body and soul, now and forevermore.

And it friggin' MYSTIFIED me that the rest of the world didn't get it! Why weren't these guys on the radio? TOP 40 radio? When the "Do You Wanna Dance"/"Babysitter" single came out in '78, I was convinced, CONVINCED that it'd be a double A-side pop radio smash. And I'm still right that it should have been; the rest of the world is wrong for not making it so.

I saw the Ramones…what? Nine times, I think. The first was in '78, on an incredible triple bill that gives me chills to consider even now: the Ramones, the Runaways, and the Flashcubes, for four bucks at a dive called the Brookside in Syracuse, NY. A little over a year later, they were back in Syracuse (at a recovering disco called Uncle Sam's), this time with an exclusive Central New York debut showing of their new movie, *Rock 'n' Roll High School*, followed by blistering live sets from the Flashcubes and the Ramones. (All for five bucks—still a bargain, inflation be damned!)

The personal importance of that second show cannot be overstated. Earlier that week, a good friend of mine had killed himself—blown his brains out, the bastard. He'd come by to visit me the very night he died, offering no clue of his intent, nothing I can pick up on even in hindsight. It crushed me, and I couldn't even bring myself to talk with anyone much about it. The night after his death, I went to see the Flashcubes play at a private party, numb, pissed-off, devastated, and determined to have a good time. I got stupid fucking drunk, the way that only emotionally charged teenagers can do, and held on to the Flashcubes's super-charged show as if my own life depended on it, and then got up to go to work the next day.

122

Never told anyone at work what had happened, never gave any reason why I was more sullen and tightlipped than usual. None of their fucking business. Went to the wake, though not the funeral. Spent a lot of time being angry and depressed.

And at the end of that hellish week, the Ramones came to town. Believe me, out of all the shows I've seen over the years, no two were more important to my sanity and well-being than the above-mentioned Flashcubes gig and that incredible Ramones show at Uncle Sam's. Lou Reed was right: My life was saved by rock 'n' roll.

The still-lingering emotional punch of that week heightens my awareness of what the Ramones (and the Flashcubes) have meant to me, but even without the tragedy, the facts remain: I would not have ever written about music professionally if not for the Ramones. Just as they inspired a DIY revolution in rock 'n' roll, they were one of the key catalysts of my first setting fingers to typewriter to pound out my thoughts on music. My first-ever piece of rock writing was a critique of the state of music in 1977, extolling the virtues of the Ramones. I still regard the Ramones as the single most exciting live band I've ever seen (at least on the days that I don't award that designation to the Flashcubes). More than any other band, even more than the Beatles, the Ramones still inspire within me a near-religious belief in the power of rock 'n' roll music. There has never been another band like them, nor will there ever be.

On July 4 of 2001, as my wife, daughter, and I were walking to our car after a fireworks display in Syracuse, my wife stopped me and asked me to listen. I didn't pick up on it at first, but slowly I began to make out the sound of Joey's unmistakable *Hey, ho, let's go!* blastin' outta someone's car speakers somewhere. It almost brought a tear to my eye. It always brings a smile to my face. I'm pretty sure it always will.

# CODA

## *Chewin' Out a Rhythm on My Bubblegum*

Joey Ramone did not live to see the Ramones become icons of pop culture. Today, the music of the Ramones is routinely heard in TV commercials and sitcom soundtracks. There was, at one point, plans for Martin Scorsese to direct a Ramones biopic, and at this writing, Netflix is developing a movie based on Joey's brother Mickey Leigh's autobiography *I Slept With Joey Ramone*, with Pete Davidson as Joey. The world has changed since the end of the seventies and the end of the century.

Although Joey passed before the Ramones' popular ascension, he was able to see the trend in that direction; he saw the magazine articles, the comments from other artists acknowledging a debt to the Ramones, and he was aware of the demand for more Ramones shows. He was too sick to consider a Ramones reunion for one more tour, or even just one more show.

Joey may have…strike that, he *probably* expected his group to be inducted into the Rock and Roll Hall of Fame, and he certainly believed they were worthy. The Ramones were first eligible for induction in 2001, the year Joey died. He passed in the spring, and the Ramones were among the winners when the Hall announced its honorees later in the year.

The induction ceremony was in 2002, as the Ramones were celebrated alongside fellow new inductees Gene Pitney, Isaac Hayes, Brenda Lee, Chet Atkins, Tom Petty and the Heartbreakers, Talking Heads, and Stax Records visionary Jim Stewart. In his speech inducting the Ramones, Pearl Jam's Eddie Vedder said, "The Ramones were our Beatles."

The Hall officially inducted Joey, Johnny, Dee Dee, Tommy, and Marky; latter-day Ramones Richie and C.J. were snubbed, in spite of Johnny's righteous insistence that they were Ramones, too. They should have been recognized as such.

In accepting the induction, Tommy said, "This means a lot to us. It meant everything to Joey." Dee Dee thanked himself. Johnny said, "God bless President Bush." A dysfunctional family to the end. Talking Heads drummer Chris Frantz was asked if the Ramones would join the Hall of Fame's traditional jam session after the awards. Frantz chuckled, and said, "The Ramones don't *jam*…!"

Dee Dee succumbed to a heroin overdose in 2002, less than three months after thanking himself at the Hall of Fame. Prostate cancer claimed Johnny in 2004. Tommy died in 2014, also taken by cancer. The four original members of the Ramones are gone, and many have joked that they're together now in the hereafter, still fighting and squabbling as they did in life.

The Ramones battled each other like brudders. But they were indeed brudders, united not by blood but by a bond unique to their experience. Some of them may have denied it, but the bond was there.

In the course of our discussion, Joey made a point of complimenting Johnny's distinctive guitar style, and he made a favorable comparison of Marky to the likes of Keith Moon and Ginger Baker. Marky was pleasantly surprised—flabbergasted, really—to hear that Joey had said that.

When Joey died, Johnny said something to the effect that he didn't like Joey, and that he couldn't understand why Joey's death depressed him. Johnny later told Ramones tour manager Monte Melnick (quoted in Melnick's book *On the Road With the Ramones*), "When Joey was alive, I thought there was always a chance that maybe the Ramones will do something, another song or something. When he died, I thought, 'Boy, that's the end of the Ramones.'

I'm not doing anything without him. I felt that was it. He was my partner. Me and him. I miss that."

In my interviews with the Ramones, Joey, Johnny, Marky, and C. J. spoke on the record. The sole instance where I was asked to take something off the record was one moment—one—when a member of the Ramones made a relatively innocuous personal observation about a bandmate. The remark was factual, and it was discussed openly and on the record by two other Ramones. Nonetheless, the Ramone making the comment thought it could seem hurtful and requested that it be deleted from the transcript. That request stands.

Brudders. Hell, *brothers*. We will never see their like again.

The few, the proud.

Semper Fi.

*Gabba Gabba Hey!*